The Passion of Man
In Gospel and Literature

David Anderson

The Bible Reading Fellowship

First published 1980

© BRF 1980

BRF Book Club no. 8

British Library CIP data

Anderson, David

The passion of man.

1. Jesus Christ – Passion   2. Tragedy

I. Title   II. Bible Reading Fellowship
232.9′6   BT431

ISBN 0-900164-53-0

design/print Eyre & Spottiswoode Ltd

Acknowledgements

I gratefully acknowledge permission from authors, translators, publishers, and other copyright holders to quote from the works stated:

C. Andrade, 'Fourth Poem'; N. de Sousa, 'The Poem of João' – tr. by Margaret Dickinson: East African Publishing House. S. Barrington-Ward, *CMS News Letter*, Dec. 1975: the author. S. Beckett, *Waiting for Godot*; T. S. Eliot, 'Four Quartets' from *Collected Poems 1909–1962*; W. Golding, *Lord of the Flies, Pincher Martin, The Spire*; G. Steiner, *The Death of Tragedy*; A. Schoenberg, *Style and Idea*: Faber & Faber Ltd. A. Camus, *The Plague*, tr. by Stuart Gilbert: Hamish Hamilton Ltd. B. Dadié, 'I thank you God' from *French African Verse*, tr. by John Reed and Clive Wake: Heinemann Educational Books Ltd. G. Ewart, 'The Name of the Game', from *New Poems 1971–2*, ed. Peter Porter, Hutchinson: P.E.N. International. E. M. Forster, *Howards End*: King's College Cambridge, and the Society of Authors. John F. X. Harriott, SJ, Article in *The Times*, 19 Feb. 1977: Times Newspapers Ltd. F. Kafka, 'In the Penal Settlement' from *In the Penal Settlement*, tr. by Willa and Edwin Muir; 'The Great Wall of China', from *Description of a Struggle and The Great Wall of China*, tr. by Willa and Edwin Muir and Tania and James Stern; T. Mann, *Doctor Faustus*, tr. by H. T. Lowe-Porter: Martin Secker & Warburg Ltd. A. Kassam, 'The Desert': Kenya Literature Bureau. A. Lewis, 'The East', from *Raiders' Dawn*: George Allen & Unwin (Publishers) Ltd. B. Pasternak, *Doctor Zhivago*, tr. by Max Hayward and Manya Harari: Collins Publishers. A. Solzhenitsyn, *The Gulag Archipelago*, tr. by Thomas P. Whitney: Collins Publishers. Sophocles, 'King Oedipus' and 'Oedipus at Colonus', from *The Theban Plays*, tr. by E. F. Watling, p. 68 lines 1524–30, p. 120 lines 1614–19, p. 121 lines 1634–50: reprinted by permission of Penguin Books Ltd. W. Soyinka, 'Purgatory', from *Poems of Black Africa*, Heinemann Educational

Books Ltd: Rex Collins. Sylvia Plath, 'Mary's Song', from *Winter Trees*, Faber: Ted Hughes, Esq. Dylan Thomas, 'Do Not Go Gentle', from *Collected Poems 1934—1952*, J. M. Dent: David Higham Associates Ltd. P. White, *Riders in the Chariot*: Jonathan Cape Ltd.

Quotations from the Bible are taken except where otherwise stated from *The New English Bible* by permission of the Delegates of the Oxford University Press and The Syndics of the Cambridge University Press.

Preface

This small book was prompted by a suggestion made by the Director of The Bible Reading Fellowship, Raymond Hammer, that I should 'throw together' some quotations from the Bible and from modern literature. I soon discovered that this apparently simple idea was very hard to put into practice. The first problem was the obvious one of selection: the Bible is a large book, and 'modern literature' produces thousands of new titles every year. After casting about for several weeks, I decided to take the Passion narrative in Mark's gospel as my biblical base and to set beside it some quotations from the Old Testament and from the literature of tragedy. This meant taking 'tragedy' to include any literature which explores and enacts the passion of man: not only the great tragic dramas of the Greeks and Shakespeare, but more especially the plays, novels and poetry of our own century in which the creative imagination negotiates the present horror of the time. My thesis is that the passion of man explored in tragic literature is the same passion as that appropriated by the Son of Man on Calvary, and that there is a comparability of meaning between the one and the other which may help us to gain a deeper understanding of the story of our redemption. This is not to say that the meaning of Calvary can be wholly expressed in terms of literary values: I have argued that the divine Word reshapes all our patterns of meaning into the saving truth of God. But the universal human reality which the incarnate Word assumed must include the human reality which the literary imagination measures and in a sense defines; and it seems reasonable to suppose that access to the one should help us to gain access to the other. Until we know Jesus as Son of Man, perhaps we cannot know him as Son of God.

Any selection from modern literature, however, must be severely limited by the knowledge and taste of the selector. Many of the books which I have strained for relevance are established twentieth-century classics which one can assume are widely read. I have already discussed a number of them in a previous book, but the treatment here is rather different. I hope that the inclusion of some African poetry will introduce readers to some fine verse which may not be familiar to them, and will also provide a welcome enlargement of the range and interest of the book as a whole.

It is seldom that a quotation conveys its full meaning in the absence of its context in the book from which it is taken, so one has to decide how much explanation is required. There is also the problem of finding a suitable balance between the literary material and the interlinking comment. I do not know whether I have got the formula right or whether obfuscation has triumphed. I hope, nevertheless, that some readers will find help here and that others will be encouraged or exasperated into doing a better job for themselves.

Hertfordshire College of Higher Education
Wall Hall, Aldenham
December 1979

for
my friends
at
Wall Hall

Contents

1: Journey

After the gift of the Spirit at Pentecost and in order to carry out the risen Christ's commission to 'proclaim the Good News to the whole creation' (Mark 16:15), the preachers and teachers of the Christian community had to find appropriate language in which to express the meaning of the life and death and resurrection of Jesus. They found that language in ideas and images which were already familiar to their hearers and readers. Most of them came from the Jewish scriptures. The writers of the documents collected in what was later called the 'New Testament' were able to assume a broad continuity of meaning between Israel's witness to God and the Christian experience of Jesus. The God who had spoken to his People of old time in the prophets had now spoken in his Son (Hebrews 1:1–2): it was the same God and initially the same People, and therefore the language of Israel's faith must be of special relevance to the new experience. So we find St Paul, for example, drawing on such Jewish ideas as law, covenant, redemption, sacrifice and so on in order to explain the saving work of Christ. The name 'Christ' was itself the Greek equivalent of the Jewish term 'Messiah'. These ideas and images carried contexts of meaning which could be related to the story of Jesus so that the new faith might be articulated and understood. The Church marked its appropriation of them by naming the Jewish scriptures the 'Old Testament'.

Although the great majority of these patterns of meaning were drawn from Jewish tradition, sources of comparison were also available from the wider culture of Greece and Rome. The writer to the Hebrews describes Jesus on a few occasions as 'the pioneer of salvation' (2:10), a 'forerunner on our behalf' (6:19), and as 'the pioneer and perfecter of our faith' (12:2, all RSV). The picture suggested by these words is that of a hero who achieves some triumph on behalf of mankind or of an athlete who wins a race and sets a new record. These models were probably of Greek rather than Jewish origin. The writer seems to be comparing Jesus to a hero of Greek mythology, and to a champion runner in the Greek games. Like them, he is saying, Jesus has won a new triumph and set a new record: he has broken through death into eternal life and has made it possible for his followers to do the same.

It is interesting to notice, however, that the one word which neither this Epistle nor the rest of the New Testament uses of Jesus is the actual word 'hero'. Perhaps it was avoided because it was too distinctively Greek, and it was felt that its use might invite too specific a comparison between Jesus and such heroes as Heracles, Prometheus, Theseus and the rest. The writer to the Hebrews may have been suggesting such a comparison, but he combined it with the Jewish model of priesthood and did not work it out in anything like the same detail. Indeed, it seems to have become important in later times to show, not that Jesus resembled the Greek heroes, but that he totally differed from them. Thus we find Athanasius, the great Christian theologian of the fourth century, arguing that Jesus could not be classed with Heracles or other heroes because none of them rose from the dead. Strictly speaking, of course, that was not altogether true of Heracles, who was represented in the story of one of his labours as returning in triumph from the Underworld having captured Cerberus. There may have been a tendency, however, among those familiar with Greek culture in the early centuries to regard Jesus as another legendary champion whose exploits were inferior to those of his Greek predecessors. But Athanasius denied that there was any continuity of meaning between Greek myth and Christian experience.[1] The context of meaning to which Jesus belonged was that of Jewish history and prophecy: he did not belong to the world of the Greek heroes.

If, however, in spite of Athanasius, we follow up the comparison suggested in the Epistle to the Hebrews, we can see that there are at least some similarities between the story of Jesus and that of the mythic or epic hero. Like the hero, Jesus accepts a destiny which requires him to journey into a kind of no-man's land and to endure an ordeal of conflict and terror in order that a treasure may be gained and a kingdom established.

Again, like the hero, he acts on behalf of the human race and his victory is an archetypal triumph which benefits mankind. In contrast, however, we can see that, although the story of Jesus is comparable in its general pattern to that of the mythic heroic journey, the differences in actual content are great. The story of Jesus is not a metaphor of human life like that of the hero: it is an historical enactment of it, a direct and explicit appropriation of human experience in its most abrasive reality. Nor is Jesus himself part God and part man in the sense in which many of the heroes were. He called upon no super-natural powers to turn aside the full assault of evil and to exempt himself from its deepest horror. His victory was not an arbitrary triumph over forces external to man: it was won within the human passion itself, within the terms of man's own failures and conflicts and afflictions. Jesus was not the agent of a mythological god whose involvement in the world was only by proxy: he was the divine Son who accepted for himself the limitations of a human life, participating in its reality without privilege or exemption, but bringing into the heart of man's darkness the light of God's self-involving love.

We might say that in the story of Jesus the myth of the heroic journey has been reshaped into a new meaning. The basic model is still recognisable, but its reshaping marks a transformation of human myth into divine truth. We might further say that no model, not even that of the Messiah of Jewish prophecy, provides an exact correlate of Jesus. All such patterns of meaning are modified by the truth of the Gospel. But those human patterns are, as it were, part of the 'flesh' which the incarnate Word informs and transfigures, part of that universal humanity which God in Christ assumed and redeemed. The context of meaning which makes possible the articulation of the Gospel is the humanity of the incarnate life of Christ himself. The transformation of meaning comes about through the divine Word which fills that humanity with the truth of God and reshapes it for our salvation.

If we think of the humanity of Christ as the context within which the Gospel is to be understood, then it seems clear that we must take that humanity in its widest possible sense. Every pattern or model of whatever age or culture which embodies the basic conflicts and resolutions of human life and imagination must have relevance to the representative humanity of Jesus as Son of Man. Although there is therefore a fundamental sense in which all such models are equal, however, there is also a sense in which some are more equal than others. Effective models are those which function as living embodiments of human experience and aspiration at specific times within particular cultures. Stories which functioned like this in earlier cultures can cease to do so in later ones. Modern analysis has revealed the profound psychological, sociological and religious significance of the mythic world; but it seems doubtful whether the stories in Homer and Hesiod, for example, can function for us today as effective figurations of man's attempts to come to terms with the polarities of his existence, though we have ample evidence in a work like James Joyce's novel *Ulysses*, for example, to show that their power as archetypes can be re-awakened by modern literary treatments. That, however, is precisely the point: although myths can die, the experiences and hopes which they embody do not die. The literary imagination can body forth new forms of things unknown, new figurations of patterns of life and meaning which the old stories no longer adequately express. That is precisely what happened in ancient Greece itself. The myths were dying, but the tragic poets embodied the pattern of the mythic journey in the greatest of all literary forms – that of the tragic poetic drama. 'It was through tragedy', says Nietzsche, 'that myth achieved its profoundest content, its most expressive form; it arose once again like a wounded warrior, its eyes alight with the unspent power and the calm wisdom of the dying' *(The Birth of Tragedy)*.

Anyone who has witnessed or simply read the classical tragedies of Aeschylus, Sophocles and Euripides knows how powerfully they still speak to us. Agamemnon and Orestes, Oedipus and Antigone, Alcestis and Hippolytus, negotiate deeper levels of our awareness than the heroes of myth. The tragic dramas of ancient Greece, like those of Shakespeare and Racine, attain a universality which transcends their time and enables them to address us across the centuries. Their stories are stories of journeys, but they are not symbolic journeys like those of the mythic heroes: the tragic hero does not grope his way under the mountain of Masu like the Sumerian hero Gilgamesh or into the centre of the Cretan labyrinth like the Greek hero Theseus; nor does he wander over the sea like Odysseus. His journey is a journey 'into the interior', into the darkness of the soul, often passing from an initial, ironic greatness into extreme reaches of experience in conflict, suffering and death. The greatness of man, the tragic poet seems to say, is always deceptive and contains within it the seeds of unforeseen disaster. The wise man will not give a verdict on his own or another's life until its full tale has been told. Thus the Chorus comments on the story of Oedipus:

> Sons and daughters of Thebes, behold: this was Oedipus,
> Greatest of men; he held the key to the deepest mysteries;
> Was envied by all his fellow men for his great prosperity;
> Behold, what a full tide of misfortune swept over his head.
> Then learn that mortal man must always look to his ending,
> And none can be called happy until that day when he carries
> His happiness down to the grave in peace.
> (Sophocles, *The Theban Plays* tr. E. F. Watling, Penguin Classics, p. 68)

The tragic poets reshaped the pattern of the heroic journey and changed its focus: the greatness of the hero is no longer that of an armed strength which, supported by the favour of the gods, triumphs over symbolic hostile forces, and the goal of his journey is not glory in this world. The tragic hero is great because he suffers greatly: he is the first agoniser or contender, the 'protagonist', of his story, and he contends with the actual guilt and horror of the time in the centre of his own being as one who bears its agony on behalf of mankind. And the end of the drama is not a manifest triumph but a sense of reconciliation in the world of spirit, as though a curse had been worked through and lifted from the human condition; and the resolution to which the drama points is that of a new vision which suffering has itself enlarged and deepened into a fuller, more inclusive wholeness.

Among the many models which may present themselves for comparison and contrast with the story of Jesus, that of tragedy, the literary enactment of the passion of man, seems to be one of the most appropriate. We may suggest that the story of Jesus reshaped a Jewish pattern of heroism in much the same way as the tragic poets reshaped that of the mythic hero. The Davidic Messiah of prophecy was essentially an epic rather than a tragic figure: he would come, in the majestic rightness of his divine cause, to defeat the enemies of the People of God and to establish a new kingdom of righteousness and glory in this world. There was no question of the Messiah's own participation in the suffering and guilt of the people. He was a figure of power whose advent would bring suffering and guilt to an end through arbitrary acts of divine intervention. Of course this would not happen until the people repented of their sins and turned to the Lord; but the picture of the Davidic Messiah persisted as an expectation of victory over earthly enemies and the setting up of an independent Jewish kingdom. Thus, in Jesus' time, religious hopes were combined with political programmes for expelling the Roman conquerors. Some notable exceptions to this existed among parties like the Essenes, whose aspirations were directed towards the attainment of a purely spiritual righteousness; but popular expectation looked for a Messiah who would defeat the enemy, and the resistance movement centred in the Zealots sought to hasten his arrival by political subversion of the Roman State.

The gospels make it clear that Jesus resisted these expectations. To him, the Messiah was not an epic but a tragic figure, and the kingdom he would establish would be the reign of God in the hearts of men. No acts of arbitrary power could establish such a kingdom: to win the hearts of men meant for Jesus an identification with the passion of man to the point of forsakenness, crucifixion and death. As in the case of the tragic hero, the focus changed from triumph over external enemies to personal involvement in the guilt and pain of mankind. The conflict of Jesus was not with political oppressors but with all that distorts and destroys the image of God in man, and that conflict took place in his own experience, in the centre of his own being. There was a more appropriate model in the Jewish tradition than that of the victorious Davidic Messiah: it was Second Isaiah's tragic Servant of the Lord, whose soul was made an offering for sin and who poured out his soul unto death (Isaiah 53:10−12).

The events of what we call 'Holy Week' begin with a scene of epic triumph which turns out to be an ironic misinterpretation of Jesus' destiny:

> And people carpeted the road with their cloaks, while others spread brushwood which they had cut in the fields; and those who went ahead and the others who came behind shouted, 'Hosanna! Blessings on him who comes in the name of the Lord! Blessings on the coming kingdom of our father David! Hosanna in the heavens!'
>
> (Mark 11:8–10)

The followers of Jesus thought that the road into Jerusalem was the path to triumphant kingship; but the throne at its end was a cross, and the crown was of thorns.

In this reversal from triumph to disaster, there is a resemblance between the story of Jesus and one of the characteristic patterns of tragic drama. As we have seen, tragedy often turns on the contrast between the initial, illusory splendour of the hero and the abyss into which he plunges. The tragic hero falls from a height, like another tragic figure of the Old Testament − Job:

> If I could only go back to the old days,
> to the time when God was watching over me,
> when his lamp shone above my head,
> and by its light I walked through the darkness!
> If I could be as in the days of my prime,
> when God protected my home,
> while the Almighty was still there at my side,
> and my servants stood round me,
> while my path flowed with milk,
> and the rocks streamed oil!
>
> (Job 29:2−6)

17

But now

> . . . my soul is in a turmoil within me,
> and misery has me daily in its grip.
> By night pain pierces my very bones,
> and there is ceaseless throbbing in my veins;
> my garments are all bespattered with my phlegm,
> which chokes me like the collar of a shirt.
> God himself has flung me down in the mud,
> no better than dust or ashes.
>
> (Job 30:16−19)

Men often persuade themselves that their routes through life are secure roads of success; but in tragedy such men are seen as the dupes of a fatal irony, because they are on a road which leads to unforeseen disaster. When Oedipus left Corinth and set out for Thebes, he thought he was walking away from the terrible destiny which the oracle had predicted; but in fact he was walking towards it; and, at a place where three roads met, unknowingly he fulfilled the first part of the prophecy by killing his own father. Sophocles' tragedy unfolds the inexorable progress of the hidden fate which determines Oedipus' destiny. In Stravinsky's musical version of the play, the orchestra repeatedly hammers out the dactylic beat of the word *trivium* as Oedipus, in the pride of his search for truth, gradually discovers the terrible meaning of the event at the three roads. So also, in the New Testament, the journey of Jesus from triumph to tragedy is seen as being inevitable and inescapable: as in the destiny of the tragic hero, there is a necessity at work which will drive the events inexorably to their conclusion. Three times in the gospel account of the last weeks of Jesus' ministry, the motif of rejection, suffering and death is emphatically repeated:

> and he began to teach them that the Son of Man had to undergo great sufferings, and to be rejected by the elders, chief priests, and doctors of the law; to be put to death, and to rise again three days afterwards. (Mark 8:31; see also 9:30−32, 10:33−34)

Unlike Oedipus, however, Jesus accepted the necessity that was laid upon him, and he walked deliberately along its path:

> I must be on my way today and tomorrow and the next day, because it is unthinkable for a prophet to meet his death anywhere but in Jerusalem. (Luke 13:33)

It was his followers who mistook the nature of the journey and who hailed him as the triumphant son of David.

In the literature of our own time, although the traditional form of the classical tragic drama is seldom used, it hardly needs saying that the tragic theme, the literary enactment of the passion of man, persists in a great variety of forms and figurations. The sense of tragic irony is especially strong in modern literature because our writers distil the experience of a century in which many confident journeys have ended in disaster and many great hopes have turned to dust and ashes. Some of our most characteristic writers today register the collapse of human hope to a kind of zero-point of despair. One of the typical figures of our time is the refugee, and one of our paradigm journeys leads to the prison camp and the gas chamber. The novelist Patrick White portrays a group of German Jews who persuade themselves that the train in which they are travelling is taking them on the first stage of a journey to Palestine. The train stops at Friedensdorf. A German voice comes over loudspeakers bidding the travellers welcome. Cheerful music is heard, and the travellers' spirits revive. Surely, they think, this must be a transit camp for rest and refreshment before they continue their journey to the Land . . .

But this delusion is soon shattered by the terrible reality. Attention! Attention! All the new arrivals must go to the bath-houses. Men will go to the left and women to the right. They must be thoroughly washed and disinfected after their journey.

A stranger speaks to Himmelfarb, one of the Jewish travellers, telling him that the women usually go in first. What do you mean? he asks. Into the gas, the stranger replies. Very soon the gas will be pouring into the bath-houses. When it is over, the bodies will be dragged to the pits. 'It suggested a harvest ritual rather than the conventions of hell.'[2]

The French novelist François Mauriac identified the gas chamber as one of the terminuses at which the metaphorical journey of Western Europe along the path of progress and enlightenment had ended:

> This foolish hope, which rushed headlong along so many routes . . . discovers today that all these routes converge on the same gas chamber, on the debris of bombed towns, on the atrociously burnt corpses of Hiroshima.

Like some of the heroes of classical tragedy, we men of hope have been the dupes of a fatal irony, and some of our best writers have compelled us to sound the depths of this awareness. In his famous novel, *The Plague*, Albert Camus depicted the shallow optimism of the citizens of Oran when the first signs of the epidemic had already become apparent. No one could believe that a frightful disease was breaking out. Although plagues are as common as wars in history, they always take people by surprise. The citizens of Oran were like everybody else: they were 'humanists' who 'disbelieved in pestilences'. So in spite of the dead rats in streets and houses, and in spite of the increasing toll among the people themselves, they carried on as usual, doing business, arranging journeys and meetings, giving no thought to the plague which was about to disrupt their lives and to cancel all journeys by sealing off Oran from the outside world.

But twentieth-century man is having to learn how to live in a world in which hopeful journeys have again and again been cancelled. At the end of his novel, Camus reminds the reader that no final redemption is ever possible. Relief from plague is never more than a temporary respite. The plague bacillus never dies or disappears for good. It lies dormant for years in furniture, among clothes and books, and in cellars. And one day, 'for the bane and enlightening of men', it will become active again and rouse up its rats and send them out of their holes 'to die in a happy city'.[3]

The 'plague' in Camus' novel is, of course, more than the

physical disease. It also represents a corruption of the soul, a will-to-power in man which is comparable to the *'hubris'* or excess of some heroes of tragedy and leads to acts of tyranny and outrage against other men. The scale, however, has been enormously extended in our time. We have learnt that hubris can corrupt whole nations, and we have seen its manifestations in two world wars and in crimes against humanity of unprecedented magnitude and horror. Nor has the full tale yet been told. We may add the normalisation of terror as a political policy of corrupt regimes, and the insane violence of revolutionary and liberation movements. And because our hopes have been pitched higher, because we have believed in the infinite progress of an enlightened age, the tragic irony has been more deeply felt. The Lament of Thomas Mann's composer Adrian Leverkühn expresses an extremity of desolation to which none of us can claim to be a stranger:

> Now only this can avail us, only this will be sung from our very souls: the Lamentation of the son of hell, the lament for men and God, issuing from the subjective, but always broadening out and as it were laying hold on the Cosmos; the most frightful lament ever set up on this earth.
> (Thomas Mann, *Doctor Faustus*, Penguin ed., p. 465)

There are many places in the world where the human journey of hope has terminated in the passion of man. Most of those places are unknown except to those who shared in or witnessed what was enacted there:

> There are on the earth 50,000 dead whom no one
>   mourned
>   on the earth
>   unburied
>   50,000 dead
> whom no one mourned
> A thousand Guernicas and the message in the
>   brush-strokes of Orozco and
>   de Signeiros
> it had the dimensions of the sea, this silence

spread across the land
   as if the rain rained blood
   as if the coarse hair was grass many meters high
   as if the mouths condemned
   in the very moment of their 50,000 deaths
   all the living of the earth
There are on the earth 50,000 dead
whom no one mourned
no one . . .
the mothers of Angola
   died together with their sons.
   ('Fourth Poem' by Costa Andrade, tr. from the Portuguese by Margaret Dickinson, *Poems of Black Africa*,
   Heinemann 1975, p. 223)

But there are some places of which almost the whole world knows. One is an ancient site in or near the old city of Jerusalem. Others are of our own century: among them are the memorials at Dachau and Auschwitz to those who died in the concentration camps, and the museum at Hiroshima which commemorates the victims of the atom bombs. The line of history which stretches between these known and unknown places is a continuous one: the Jesus of the cross on Calvary is also the Jesus of Auschwitz and Hiroshima and Angola, and the darkness of his noon is the darkness of our own.

[1] 'De Incarnatione', *Library of Christian Classics vol. III*, pp. 69, 100–105.
[2] P. White, *Riders in the Chariot*, Penguin ed., pp. 179–183.
[3] A. Camus, *The Plague*, Penguin ed., pp. 34, 252.

2: Agony, Arrest, Trial

Agony

> When they reached a place called Gethsemane, he said to his disciples, 'Sit here while I pray.' And he took Peter and James and John with him. Horror and dismay came over him, and he said to them, 'My heart is ready to break with grief; stop here, and stay awake.' Then he went forward a little, threw himself on the ground, and prayed that, if it were possible, this hour might pass him by. 'Abba, Father,' he said, 'all things are possible to thee; take this cup away from me. Yet not what I will, but what thou wilt.' (Mark 14:32−36)

The language of the agony expresses deep intensity of feeling. Jesus was no detached hero, able to survey his fate from a calm Olympian height; nor was he a willing martyr seeking post-humous glory for his cause. His words suggest loss of direction, a mental and spiritual disorientation. The ministry of God's healing, life-giving work among men had failed in the place of greatest challenge − Jerusalem. What had happened now to the confident reply to the Baptist's question, 'Are you the one who is to come, or are we to expect some other?'

> 'Go and tell John what you hear and see: the blind recover their sight, the lame walk, the lepers are made clean, the deaf hear, the dead are raised to life, the poor are hearing the good news − and happy is the man who does not find me a stumbling-block.' (Matthew 11:4−6)

There was no sign in Gethsemane of the blessedness which had surrounded the gospel mission when the people 'heard him gladly'. Even his closest friends failed him and slept. The agony was the first stage of an increasing isolation which left

Jesus abandoned by man and God. Events were moving towards the final contradiction of those signs of the kingdom to which Jesus had pointed in the days of triumph:

> '. . . if it is by the finger of God that I drive out the devils, then be sure the kingdom of God has already come upon you.' (Luke 11:20)

The Father's will had become opaque to Jesus. The darkness of Gethsemane anticipated the intenser darkness of Calvary. In the Garden, Jesus could still say, 'Thy will be done', in spite of his agony of doubt. But on Calvary even that consolation was to be taken from him.

> The night was a kingdom of annihilation,
> Of non-being,
> The whole world seemed uninhabited,
> And only this garden was a place for the living.
>
> He gazed into the black abyss,
> Empty, without beginning or end.
> Sweating blood, he prayed to his Father
> That this cup of death should pass him by.
> (from 'Gethsemane', B. Pasternak, *Doctor Zhivago*,
> Collins Fontana ed., p. 538)

Jesus had recognised the inevitability of his condemnation and death. But it is one thing to anticipate something, and quite another to be prepared for it when it comes. The agony in the Garden was a wrenching re-centring of mind and soul around the horrors of rejection, torture and death. There was to be no reprieve: the question now was whether there could be a meaningful acceptance of events which were a total negation of all that had gone before.

> In the days of his earthly life he offered up prayers and petitions, with loud cries and tears, to God who was able to deliver him from the grave. Because of his humble submission his prayer was heard: son though he was, he

learned obedience in the school of suffering . . .
(Hebrews 5:7–8)

The agony in Gethsemane, with its metaphor of drinking the cup of suffering and its sweat of blood, has become a widely appropriated image of the passion of man. The intensity of Jesus' disappointment and darkness of soul; his anguished longing to find a way of avoiding the horror that awaited him; his final acceptance of the dark mystery of the Father's will — all this has burnt into the consciousness of men and women wherever the story of Jesus is known. The scene in the Garden surpasses in tragic intensity any drama of the literary imagination, and has itself become a figuration which gives, as it were, a local habitation and a name to the general universe of woe. Here, for example, is Arnold Schoenberg using the image of Gethsemane to express the self-doubt which assailed Mahler in the face of hostile criticism of his music:

Gustav Mahler was a saint.
Anyone who knew him even slightly must have had that feeling. Perhaps only a few understood it. And even among those few, only the men of good will honoured him. The others reacted to the saint as evil has always reacted to goodness and greatness: they martyred him. They carried things so far that this good man doubted his own work. Not once was the cup allowed to pass away from him. Even the bitterest he had to drink: the loss, if only temporary, of faith in his work. How will they seek to justify themselves when they are accused of having brought one of the greatest composers of all time to the point where he was deprived of the sole, the highest recompense for a creative mind, the recompense found when the artist's faith in himself allows him to say, 'I have not been in error'? (A. Schoenberg, *Style and Idea*, new ed., Faber 1975, p. 447)

The Jesus of Gethsemane is present for all who have contended with failure and self-doubt. He is present in the extreme experiences of men and women whose world has collapsed into 'the dark backward and abysm of time' and for whom the future seems full of horror. He is present as the companion of our sorrow and its most tragic exemplar. But he is also present as its redeemer. He rose from his agony having 'gazed into the black abyss' and having seen in it the form of the Father's will. The darkness was not dispelled: it was to become even more intense in a darkness which covered the whole earth. But it could not overcome the light of life:

> All that came to be was alive with his life, and that life was the light of men. The light shines on in the dark, and the darkness has never mastered it. (John 1:4−5)

The Welsh poet Alun Lewis, who was killed in the second world war, formulated the question which Gethsemane asks and which the resurrection answers:

> 'If passion and grief and pain and hurt
> Are but the anchorite's hair-shirt,
> Can such a torment of refining
> Be aimless wholly, undesigning?
> Must
> Such aching
> Go to making
> Dust?'
> Whispered the wind in the olive tree
> In the garden of Gethsemane.
> (Alun Lewis, 'The East', in *Raiders' Dawn*, Allen & Unwin 1942)

Arrest

> Suddenly, while he was still speaking, Judas, one of the Twelve, appeared, and with him was a crowd armed with swords and cudgels, sent by the chief priests, lawyers, and elders. Now the traitor had agreed with them upon a signal: 'The one I kiss is your man; seize him and get him

safely away.' When he reached the spot, he stepped forward at once and said to Jesus, 'Rabbi', and kissed him. Then they seized him and held him fast.

One of the party drew his sword, and struck at the High Priest's servant, cutting off his ear. Then Jesus spoke: 'Do you take me for a bandit, that you have come out with swords and cudgels to arrest me? Day after day I was within your reach as I taught in the temple, and you did not lay hands on me. But let the scriptures be fulfilled.' Then the disciples all deserted him and ran away.

(Mark 14:43–50)

Jesus was arrested by night in an unfrequented place. He was betrayed by one of his closest followers who identified him with a kiss, and was marched away by a motley crowd of armed underlings who were carrying out the orders of the Jewish authorities. One of his friends (perhaps Peter as in John 18:10) put up a token resistance, but finally they 'all deserted him and ran away'.

The arrest of Jesus has many of the classic ingredients of the political arrest. It was done as secretly as possible to avoid 'confrontation'. Judas' part was to keep track of Jesus and inform the authorities of his whereabouts so that the arrest could be made at a convenient place and time 'without collecting a crowd' (Luke 22:6). The disciples, having just awakened from sleep, were off guard and uncertain what to do. It was all over in a few moments.

Such arrests have been well documented in our own time, and they all have a markedly similar pattern. Betrayal, secrecy, surprise, speed – these are their characteristic features; but, as befits our progressive age, everything is now done with far greater efficiency. Arrest by night, as Solzhenitsyn tells us, is a favourite with the authorities. People are in bed, they are not prepared for the sudden knock on the door. The arrested man is dazed with sleep and struggles into his trousers hardly knowing what he is doing. At night, there is very little chance that a crowd of people will gather to challenge the security police. The arrests can be carried out methodically, one by one, on successive nights, and few people, apart from the arrested persons and their families, will be any the wiser.

But to the arrested man himself, arrest is a breaking point in his life. It is like a bolt of lightning or an earthquake. His whole universe is shattered when the police hiss at him, *You are under arrest.* Yet the mind cannot grasp the reality of what has happened: it cannot believe that life is now irrevocably changed. All that the arrested man can think of saying is, 'Me? What for?' That is the question which has been asked a million times. But it has yet to receive an answer.[1]

The gospel record portrays Jesus at the moment of his arrest as outwardly calm and unsurprised. His 'hour' has come and he accepts it without resistance. But arrest is really never something a man can simply take in his stride: for Jesus, as for others, it must have been a displacement of his universe, with the question 'Why?' unanswered. As an act of men against one who had challenged lawful authority, perhaps the arrest was understandable; indeed, Jesus seems to have thought that it would have happened earlier when he was teaching in the temple. But as an act of God against one who had proclaimed his nearness and his grace, it was the edge of a dark and shattering mystery.

It was hardly less shattering for the disciples and followers of Jesus. Mark tells us that they all ran away, and later he gives us the poignant scene of Peter's denial. The account suggests the kind of total confusion that comes over men when the bottom suddenly drops out of their world. Jesus had been 'a prophet powerful in speech and action before God and the whole people' (Luke 24:19). His followers 'had been hoping that he was the man to liberate Israel' (Luke 24:21). Perhaps the disciples' feelings were like those expressed by the Mozambique poet Noémia de Sousa, mourning the arrest of a modern hero who had kindled hope:

> João was young like us
> João had wideawake eyes
> and alert ears
> hands reaching forwards
> a mind cast for tomorrow
> a mouth to cry an eternal 'no'
> João was young like us . . .

João longed to live and conquer life
that is why he loathed prisons, cages, bars
and loathed the men who make them.
For João was free
João was an eagle born to fly
João loathed prisons and the men who make them
João was young like us . . .

Ah, this is why we have lost João
why we weep night and day for João
for João whom they have stolen from us.

And we ask
But why have they taken João,
João who was young and ardent like us
João who thirsted for life
João who was brother to us all
why have they stolen from us João
who spoke of hope and dawning days
João whose glance was like a brother's hug
João who always had somewhere for one of us to stay
João who was our mother and our father
João who would have been our saviour
João whom we loved and love
João who belongs so surely to us
oh, why have they stolen João from us?
and no one answers
indifferent, no one answers . . .

(from 'The Poem of João' by Noémia de Sousa, tr. from
the Portuguese by Margaret Dickinson, *Poems of Black
Africa*, p. 197)

Trial

The gospel accounts of the examination of Jesus before the
Jewish Sanhedrin and his trial before Pilate are brief sum-
maries of what were probably quite lengthy proceedings, and
it is impossible to make of them a consistent, wholly intellig-
ible record. One element which the tradition has preserved is
the silence of Jesus before his judges. Answers to questions
seem to have been wrung from him unwillingly, and they

were apparently equivocal and ambiguous. There is a remoteness about Jesus in the trial scenes, contrasting strongly with the intimacy of Gethsemane, and the gospel record does not give us access to his feelings.

But we must surely reject the view that Jesus' attitude was that of a superior being who was untouched by the human antics of his accusers and judges. It is hard to believe that Jesus, a loyal Jew, was unaffected by the charge of subverting the religious faith of his own people. What is quite certain, however, is that he did not behave in the least like a political revolutionary. Revolutionaries do not remain silent in court: they make speeches in which they accuse the judges of being the agents of a corrupt, oppressive regime which the new movement will sweep away. Jesus, like many Jews of his time, expected the coming of God's new age; but he did not share the Zealots' understanding of it as a political kingdom dependent upon armed rebellion. So he made no speeches from the dock when Pilate invited him to reply to the charge of subversion, and his replies to questions could hardly have been more brief. It is hard to imagine anyone less like a political revolutionary, though that was the charge which the Jewish Sanhedrin handed up to Pilate's court and on which Jesus was condemned to the Roman death of crucifixion.

But it is clear that the real Jewish charge against Jesus was that of blasphemy. He had endangered the faith and therefore the existence of Israel by unorthodox teaching. That was an offence of the utmost gravity. The very existence of Israel as the People of God was bound up with the covenanted Law of God. A teacher whose words or deeds incited people to break the Law was laying the nation open to the possibility of divine judgment. The penalty for such an offence was death (Deuteronomy 13:5, 18:20).

We may notice the paradox of the gospel story at this point. Jesus is accused of blasphemy against God, but it is God who wills that his Son should suffer and die; and the human means by which Jesus' destiny is initiated is the Sanhedrin's verdict of blasphemy. It may be that the silence of Jesus in the face of this charge, his refusal to answer even the high priest's questions about his teaching (John 18:19−21), indicate an uncertainty and even perhaps a sense of profound bewilderment. Perhaps Jesus, like Jeremiah among the prophets of old, found himself questioning the very basis of his prophetic ministry:

> O Lord, thou hast duped me, and I have been thy dupe;
> thou hast outwitted me and hast prevailed.
> I have been made a laughing-stock all the day long,
> everyone mocks me.
> Whenever I speak I must needs cry out
> and proclaim violence and destruction.
> I am reproached and mocked all the time
> for uttering the word of the Lord.
>
> (Jeremiah 20:7−8)

Jeremiah had spoken of the judgment of God against his backsliding people; Jesus had revealed the grace and love of God even to the outcasts of society. Both men criticised the religious leaders of their time and both aroused official opposition. Jeremiah was put in the stocks and imprisoned in a pit; Jesus, by a far greater irony, was handed over to the occupying power and condemned to death.

One of the classic novels of our century is entitled 'The Trial'. It is by the enigmatic Czech writer, Franz Kafka. The title is itself paradoxical, because the one thing that never occurs in the novel is a legal trial of the accused man. Joseph K, its central character, is visited one morning at his lodgings by the police and told that he is under arrest − though the police do not actually take him away. But he never discovers the nature of the charge against him, and he never appears before a judge. The legal apparatus to which he looks for justice is a sham, and the Law itself is barred to him. He is condemned for an unknown crime by a judge he has never seen in a high court to which he has never penetrated, and in the end he dies 'like a dog' at the hands of two mindless executioners. These clownish men seize K in the street and drag him off to a quarry. Suddenly, K's glance falls on an adjoining house: there is a light in one of the upstairs windows, and as he watches the window is opened and a vaguely human figure leans out towards him, stretching out its arms. Is it a friend? A good man? A rescuer? Or is it mankind come to witness K's execution like an audience in a theatre? K raises his arms and spreads out his fingers in a desperate gesture. But his rescuer − if he is a rescuer − is too late. One of the men grasps K by the throat while the other stabs him to the heart with a knife and turns the blade twice. They stand together and watch him die. 'Like a dog', says K. 'It was as if the shame of it must outlive him.'[2]

Various commentators on Kafka's novel have tried to pin a number of moral failings and misdemeanours on Joseph K. It is true that K is by no means an innocent man, but there is no suggestion in the novel that the unknown crime of which he is accused has anything to do with his minor offences, and the efforts of the commentators, who are determined that K shall be proved to be guilty of *something*, only put us in mind of similar efforts made by the friends of Job. Such explanations simply miss the point. The trial of man, Kafka seems to say, has very little to do with the plusses and minusses of ethical and legal judgments. What is at stake here is *the total meaning and value of a man's life*. In one of his 'parables', Kafka wrote:

> We are sinful not merely because we have eaten of the Tree of Knowledge, but also because we have not yet eaten of the Tree of Life. The state in which we find ourselves is sinful, quite independent of guilt.
> (F. Kafka, *Parables and Paradoxes*, Schocken Books, New York 1961, p. 29)

But the way to the Tree of Life is barred to man, and his very existence in the world is unjustified. Joseph K has committed no crime of which a human court could find him guilty. But what of the total meaning of a man's life? What of salvation and damnation? Is there a Judge who can give a verdict at the end of that trial, and where, if he exists at all, is such a Judge to be found?

There is an important scene in Kafka's novel where Joseph K meets the official court painter whose job is to turn out portraits of the judges. K questions the painter about the legal procedures. The judge, he is told, can grant an acquittal with an easy mind. Then there will only be a bit of legal tidying up to be done, and K can walk out of the court a free man. But of course there is a catch. K will be only 'provisionally' or 'ostensibly' free. The judge has no power to grant a final acquittal. That power is reserved for the highest Court of all, which is quite inaccessible to K, the painter, and everybody else. No one knows what are the prospects 'up there', and, the painter adds, no one really wants to know.[3]

Man's final acquittal is a verdict on his whole life, a justification of his human existence and of the meanings and values he has created or helped to maintain. But he is not the judge in his own trial: he cannot pronounce the final verdict of salvation or damnation on his own case. That verdict can be pronounced only by the Judge who presides over 'the highest Court of all', and twentieth-century man has no access to that Court. So his existence remains unjustified − he is sinful independently of guilt − because he is cut off from the transcendent source of meanings and values which alone can vindicate his life.

Again we are reminded of Job. Like Joseph K, Job demands a trial, the chance to state his case and have his innocence vindicated against a secret accusation of which he has not been informed:

> If only I knew how to find him,
> how to enter his court,
> I would state my case before him
> and set out my arguments in full;
> then I should learn what answer he would give
> and find out what he had to say.
>
> (Job 23:3−5)

But like Kafka's tragic hero, Job has no access to the Supreme Judge:

> If I go forward, he is not there;
> if backward, I cannot find him;
> when I turn left, I do not descry him;
> I face right, but I see him not.
>
> (Job 23:8−9)

The truth is that no human court can pronounce a safe verdict on the value and meaning of a man's life, because the real trial of man takes place in those inner recesses of mind and soul where the court has no competence. The legalism of Job's friends simply fails to engage with the interior reality of Job's case, and Kafka's Joseph K never appears before a human court at all. But both men are on trial: they seek justification of their lives in a world in which they are sinful independently of guilt. Neither of them can justify himself: each recognises his dependence upon an order of meanings and values which transcends the world in which his sinful, unjustified existence occurs. In the end, Job is granted an overwhelming vision of the Creator-God, repents of the presumption of his claims, and is rewarded with twice as much as he had before; but Joseph K, a kind of modern Job, sees only a distant, undefined human figure − before he dies, without vindication, 'like a dog'.

Jesus was brought to trial before Pilate on a trumped-up political charge which Pilate himself recognised as false. The silence of Jesus, his disinclination to defend himself against the charge of political subversion, suggests that this human trial did not engage the central reality of his being. The real trial was about the value and meaning of his life and of the Gospel of God to which his life had been dedicated. The Jewish accusation of blasphemy may have affected Jesus more deeply than the record suggests: he had to face the possibility, like Jeremiah before him, that he had been mistaken, that his gospel was a delusion. Events had demolished the old securities of the gospel ministry, and perhaps those securities had always been ill-founded or too easily assumed. What Jesus had to face was 'a new and shocking valuation' of all he had been, a sense of abandonment which put in question the very foundation on which his life and ministry had rested.

After his trial and condemnation, the soldiers mocked Jesus before they led him to Calvary. Mark tells us that they dressed him in a purple garment representing kingship, and put a crown of thorns on his head. Matthew adds that they put a stick in his hand, representing kingly authority. They paid mock homage to him, spat at him, and struck him on the head. Mark also records an earlier mocking after the decision of the

Sanhedrin to send him for trial. The Jews blindfolded Jesus and asked him to 'prophesy' which of them had struck him.

To the Jews, Jesus was a false Messiah; to the Roman soldiers, he was a bogus king. So they mocked him in different ways according to their different estimates of him. Men have continued to dress Jesus in clothes of their own choosing and then to jeer because the clothes do not fit. Satirical portraits of Jesus in our own time have followed the example of the Jews and Romans. But perhaps Jesus is also mocked by those who would have him protected from mockery. The Son of Man had no privileged status, no reputation or dignity to be preserved: his vocation was one of total vulnerability to the passion of man. He did not hide his face from shame and spitting, and it was in the final humiliation of Calvary that the Roman centurion recognised a son of God. So we do not need to tremble for Jesus when he is misrepresented and ridiculed. We might do better to tremble for ourselves. How shall *we* fare in the Trial of Man?

> For when men have once been enlightened, when they have had a taste of the heavenly gift and a share in the Holy Spirit, when they have experienced the goodness of God's word and the spiritual energies of the age to come, and after all this have fallen away, it is impossible to bring them again to repentance; for with their own hands they are crucifying the Son of God and making mock of his death.
>
> (Hebrews 6:4−6)

[1] A. Solzhenitsyn, *The Gulag Archipelago*, Collins Fontana ed., pp. 3−7.
[2] F. Kafka, *The Trial*, Secker & Warburg revised definitive ed. 1956, pp. 254−255.
[3] *The Trial*, pp. 176−177.

3: Outside the Gate

The gospel record tells us that the journey to Calvary involved a going out from the city of Jerusalem. The place of a skull lay outside the walled city in a kind of no-man's land. The writer of the Epistle to the Hebrews interprets this 'going out' of Jesus in terms of the disposal of the sin-offering 'outside the camp':

> As you know, those animals whose blood is brought as a sin-offering by the high priest into the sanctuary, have their bodies burnt outside the camp, and therefore Jesus also suffered outside the gate, to consecrate the people by his own blood. Let us then go to him outside the camp, bearing the stigma that he bore.
>
> (Hebrews 13:11–13)

The sin-offering in ancient Israel was burnt outside the camp in the place 'where the ashes are poured out' (Leviticus 4:11−12 RSV); as the bearer of human sin, the animal had become unclean and it was therefore disposed of in waste ground. So also Jesus died in a place of rejection, outside the community bounded by the walls of Jerusalem, bearing the reproach of the outcast and alien. Thus the Jesus of Calvary is identified with another aspect of the passion of man: the isolation of those who are banished to the margins of life by a world which condemns and rejects them:

> He was despised, he shrank from the sight of men,
> tormented and humbled by suffering;
> we despised him, we held him of no account,
> a thing from which men turn away their eyes . . .
> Without protection, without justice, he was taken away;
> and who gave a thought to his fate,
> how he was cut off from the world of living men,
> stricken to the death for my people's transgression?
>
> (Isaiah 53:3, 8)

Like Israel of old, exiled in Babylon as a sin-offering for the nations, Jesus went out from Jerusalem into a no-man's—land. He had been 'set at nought', he had been written off, he no longer counted.

The Romans had condemned Jesus for political reasons: he was a potential danger to the State. The marginal men and women of our own time include the political prisoners who inhabit the no-man's land of the labour camps which, in Russia, Solzhenitsyn has named 'the Gulag Archipelago':

> And the Kolyma was the greatest and most famous island, the pole of ferocity of that amazing country of Gulag which, though scattered in an Archipelago geographically, was, in the psychological sense, fused into a continent — an almost invisible, almost imperceptible country inhabited by the zek people.
> (A. Solzhenitsyn, *The Gulag Archipelago*, Fontana ed., p. ix)

There are few countries in the world today which are without their quotas of 'zeks' or prisoners of conscience who have been banished to camps and gaols. These are not the fanatics who have done deeds of cruelty and horror in the name of some political absolute; they are the people who have struggled against injustice and oppression without compromising their own humanity or outraging that of others. The Nigerian poet Wole Soyinka describes the living death of men who have entered 'the valley of the shadow of Night':

> And some have walked to the edge of the valley
> Of the shadow; and, at a faint stir in memories
> Long faded to the moment of the miracle of reprieve
> To a knowledge of rebirth and a promise of tomorrows
> And tomorrows and an ever beginning of tomorrows
> The mind retreats behind a calloused shelter
> Of walls, self-sensor[1] on the freedom of remembrance
> Tempering visions of opaque memory, to rings
> Of iron spikes, a peace of refuge passionless
> And comfort of gelded sanity.

Weaned from the moment of death, the miracle
Dulled, their minds dissolve in vagueness, a look
Empty as all thoughts are featureless which
Plunge to that lone abyss – And
Had it there ended? Had it all ended, there
Even in the valley of the shadow of Night?
(from 'Purgatory', in Poems of Black Africa, p. 108)

Soyinka's poem alludes to the valley of the shadow of death of the twenty-third Psalm: the prisoners have been reprieved from death, but they have entered 'the valley of the shadow of Night' – the emptiness and despair of those who are cut off from the land of the living 'behind a calloused shelter of walls'. The 'tomorrows' of the poem echo the 'tomorrow, and tomorrow, and tomorrow' of the famous speech in *Macbeth*; but while Soyinka sees 'tomorrow' as a promise of 'rebirth', Shakespeare's tragic vision sees only a tale

> Told by an idiot, full of sound and fury,
> Signifying nothing.
(Act V scene 5)

Along this tragic perspective, the whole world appears as a no-man's land in which there is no affirmation of being or value, nothing to give a man a sense that his existence has meaning; his entire life, from birth to death, is a write-off, and might as well never have happened at all. We meet this wholly negative verdict again in Beckett's play *Waiting for Godot*:

> Have you not done tormenting me with your accursed time? It's abominable. When! When! One day, is that not enough for you, one day like any other day, one day he went dumb, one day I went blind, one day we'll go deaf, one day we were born, one day we'll die, the same day, the same second, is that not enough for you? They give birth astride of a grave, the light gleams an instant, then it's night once more.
(S. Beckett, *Waiting for Godot*, Faber paperback ed., p. 89)

Later in the same scene, one of the tramps says:

> Astride of the grave and a difficult birth. Down in the
> hole, lingeringly, the grave-digger puts in the forceps.
>
> (p. 91)

The same tragic perspective and a very similar image of it are
present in Job's question:

> Why didst thou bring me out of the womb?
> O that I had ended there and no eye had seen me,
> that I had been carried from the womb to the grave
> and were as though I had not been born.
>
> (Job 10:18–19)

And also in Jeremiah's:

> A curse on the man who brought word to my father,
> 'A child is born to you, a son',
> and gladdened his heart! . . .
> because death did not claim me before birth,
> and my mother did not become my grave,
> her womb great with me for ever.
>
> (Jeremiah 20:15, 17)

To the writer of 'Ecclesiastes', the world and man's life in it is
an endless agitation which always returns to its starting-point
and never attains fulfilment:

> What does a man gain from all his labour and his toil here
> under the sun? Generations come and generations go,
> while the earth endures for ever.
>
> The sun rises and the sun goes down; back it returns to
> its place and rises there again. The wind blows south, the
> wind blows north, round and round it goes and returns
> full circle. All streams run into the sea, yet the sea never
> overflows; back to the place from which the streams ran
> they return to run again.
>
> All things are wearisome; no man can speak of them all.

Is not the eye surfeited with seeing, and the ear sated with hearing? What has happened will happen again, and what has been done will be done again, and there is nothing new under the sun.

(Ecclesiastes 1:3–9)

The despairing statements of Job and Jeremiah are verdicts on their individual lives which arose from personal experiences of loss and inner conflict. The verdict passed by the author of Ecclesiastes, however, is a negative judgment on human life in general: all existence occurs in an alien world in which man searches in vain for affirmation and fulfilment. Prince and beggar, wise man and fool, young and old – all discover in the end that their lives are devoid of meaning and that every aspiration is nullified by death.

This sense of what the author of Ecclesiastes calls the 'vanity' of life is one which finds particularly intense expression among some characteristic writers of our own time. Camus echoes Ecclesiastes in registering the absurdity of existence in a world in which man feels himself to be a stranger. So long as we can explain the world and human life in terms of such reassuring beliefs as the will of God, divine judgment, life after death, and so on, we are provided with a framework of meaning which makes the world familiar. But when such beliefs collapse, when man is 'suddenly deprived of illusions and light', then the world takes on an alien aspect and man feels that he is divorced from the setting in which his existence occurs. He is like Sisyphus in the Greek myth, condemned to roll a huge rock to the top of a mountain only to have it slip from his grasp and roll back to the bottom. The laborious toil is endless, and in such a world man is always a stranger. Like the author of Ecclesiastes, Camus was struck by the never-ending return of nature and of human life to their starting-points – the failure of existence to achieve permanent value. There is only one rational way of living in an absurd world: to abandon the hopeless quest for definitive meanings and to live, like nature itself, in a state of moral indifference. Meursault, the 'Outsider' in Camus' novel of that name, with the prospect of execution before him, recognises the unreality of his own life and the deluded state of the official representatives of law and religion who believe themselves to be the ministers of eternal values. Against the hard certainty of his coming death, Meursault's life seems to have been made up of haphazard choices which could easily have been different. People had tried to foist on him their ideas about life — principles, values, codes of conduct. But Meursault's execution will prove that they were wrong: nothing in human life is of the least importance. Meursault had not wept at his mother's funeral, he had refused promotion at work, he had treated his girl-friend with indifference, he had killed an Arab. But his death will 'justify' his lack of moral commitment by proving that life has no meaning and that one action is neither better nor worse than any other. So Meursault rejects the official world of delusion and pretence in favour of the world of nature, which has no concern with the supposed meanings and values of man's useless struggle. He looks up at the stars which he can see through the window of his cell, and for the first time in his life he opens his heart to 'the benign indifference of the universe'; he realises that he has been happy — his life has resembled that of the stars themselves, untroubled by moral principles and obligations, indifferent to the questions of meaning and value with which men needlessly torment and delude themselves. So Meursault's last hope is that, on the day of his execution, there will be a great crowd of spectators and that they will greet his appearance on the scaffold 'with howls of execration'.[2]

The writer of Ecclesiastes was wearied by a world which seemed to contain no affirmation or reinforcement of man's longing for attainment, but Camus' Outsider finds consolation in such a world precisely because it makes all value-judgments futile. The moral struggle can be abandoned and life can be enjoyed as existence untroubled by reflection. There is perhaps some justification for Camus' rather startling statement in his preface to the American edition of *The Outsider* that Meursault is 'the only kind of Christ we deserve'. Only Meursault is clear-sighted enough to perceive that the time-worn formulas of religion and morals entirely fail to negotiate the basic absurdity of human life, and he is heroic enough to bear on behalf of mankind the full implications of this discovery. The belief that human life has meaning and that there are some human beings who know what it is, has been shown to be a delusion. We may not 'deserve' a divine saviour, but at least Meursault has uncovered the essential truth that makes salvation necessary: that man is an alien in a senseless world, and that his banal attempts to dispel absurdity are as devoid of meaning as the world in which his pointless existence occurs.

When Jesus was being led from Jerusalem to Calvary, St Luke tells us that he turned and spoke to the weeping women who were following him:

> 'Daughters of Jerusalem, do not weep for me; no, weep for yourselves and your children. For the days are surely coming when they will say, "Happy are the barren, the wombs that never bore a child, the breasts that never fed one." Then they will start saying to the mountains, "Fall on us", and to the hills, "Cover us." For if these things are done when the wood is green, what will happen when it is dry?' (Luke 23:28–31)

Jesus' prophecy is usually taken to refer to the disaster of AD 70 when Jerusalem fell before the Roman army under Titus. He is saying that the present security of Jerusalem, supposedly the guardian city of the highest religious and moral values, is a false security, and that its rejection of himself signals the advent of its own destruction.[3] But these words of Jesus also open up a wider perspective along which life as a whole is seen in terms of spiritual barrenness and waste. Men will say that it would be better not to have been born into such a world, and they will call on nature to hide the shame of their existence in it. The 'green tree' of apparent fecundity and fulfilment is already in reality the 'dry tree' of sterility and despair.

Did Jesus himself, on that short march outside the gate from Jerusalem to Calvary, feel that his own life had been sterile and fruitless? Perhaps in bidding the women not to weep for him he was rejecting their attempt to cast him in a tragic role.[4] But his bitter words do not sound like those of a man who was satisfied with his labour under the sun, and Christian tradition has named his path to Calvary the *Via Dolorosa* and has pictured him staggering and falling under the weight of the cross he was compelled to carry. That weight has been understood, not only as a crushing physical burden, but also as a crushing burden on Jesus' spirit — the burden of human sin which Jesus bore. If we ask whether Jesus felt a despairing sense of the 'vanity' or 'absurdity' of human life as he bore his cross to Calvary, then we must say that he probably did. He had become an exile, a stranger for whom the habitual securities had collapsed and whose spirit was alienated from the Father's affirming love. That is the nature of sin, and Jesus as Son of Man accepted its full implications for himself — the nihilating isolation of a soul lost in a barren land. Some lines by a modern Kenyan poet, Amin Kassam, express this extremity of feeling: the garden of life is a mirage in a sterile desert, and the soul's thirst is mocked by dry water:

> hear my burning cry o heavens!
> hear the lament of a disillusioned soul
> whose footsteps weave drunkenly
> across the desert floor . . .
> you have seen me crawl towards
> dry scintillant water
> and yet beneath your relentless gaze
> i still plead,
> plead but for a drop! . . .
> hear my whisper o heavens
> before i fall
> i have not the strength
> to thunder forth my words
> in this land ravaged of hope
> where bleached bones seem to say
> despair of escape . . .
> perhaps there is no return.
> (from 'The Desert', *Poems of Black Africa*, p. 338)

The poet's device of using a small letter for the first person singular seems to emphasise his feeling of helplessness: it is as though he no longer has the courage or the strength to fight for his identity in a hostile, life-devouring world. Even the desert cactus, he says in a striking image, 'raises hinged arms aloft in supplication'.

This is a very different image of nature from that of Camus' Outsider. A world without love, as Rieux says in Camus' later novel *The Plague*, is a dead world. Meursault is himself deluded in supposing that a man can live in terms of 'the benign indifference of the universe', without values, meaning, or hope. An absurd world is not a pleasant garden in which we can exist as lotus-eaters: that kind of world was lost when Adam and Eve were expelled from paradise. An absurd world is a desert, a wilderness in which there is no fulfilment, nothing to give a man the feeling that his existence matters or that his solitude can be overcome. It is the 'dry tree' of Jesus' words to the women of Jerusalem − sterile, shameful, and deathly.

Spiritual deserts, like physical ones, are nearly always man-made. They can result from the self-created exile of a man's interpretation of reality in terms of his own lusts, his attempts to draw the whole of that reality into himself and to recreate it in his own image. A number of important modern writers have explored this kind of exile, but perhaps few have done so more convincingly than William Golding in his novel *Pincher Martin*. It is ostensibly a story about a man battling for survival on a rock in the middle of the Atlantic after his ship has been torpedoed. Pincher's solitude is total: his no-man's land is surrounded by the vast waste of the ocean far away from shipping-routes. But the solitude of the rock is a symbol of the isolation of Pincher's soul: for Pincher is in fact dead, and the rock is his own invention. We learn that in his past life he has been a kind of predator who has consumed other people to feed his own lusts. He has always lived in a no-man's land of self-centredness, but in death his solitude is absolute and the centre of consciousness has to invent a circumference to locate its own existence. The circumference Pincher invents is the rock, and there he struggles, grimly and even heroically, to exist.

Pincher's rock betrays occasional signs of its illusory nature, but it is not until the penultimate chapter of the novel that the illusion is shattered. A great storm blows up, and against its terrifying blackness the rock 'was proved to be as insubstantial as the painted water. Pieces went and there was no more than an island of papery stuff round the claws and everywhere else there was the mode that the centre knew as nothing.' Finally, the lightning creeps towards Pincher's hands and into the centre of his being:

> The lightning came forward. Some of the lines pointed to the centre, waiting for the moment when they could pierce it. Others lay against the claws, playing over them, prying for a weakness, wearing them away in a compassion that was timeless and without mercy.
> (William Golding, *Pincher Martin*, Faber paperback ed., p. 201)

Before the black lightning strikes him, Pincher has a conversation with God. He is now face to face with the one reality which cannot be 'consumed', which invites him to consider the hell he has created and to make a free surrender of his isolated, distorted selfhood. But Pincher will not surrender, and so the absolute lightning moves in to penetrate his being, to burn away his invented self in the consuming fire of God's merciless compassion.

There is something titanic in Pincher's determination to cling to the reality he has invented and to defy the God who offers him heaven as a reward for submission. Pincher sees himself as a Prometheus or an Ajax hurling defiance at the gods, or as King Lear calling upon the storm to do its worst:

> 'I have a right to live if I can!' he says to God.
> 'Where is that written?'
> 'Then nothing is written.'
> 'Consider.'
> He raged on the cardboard rock before the immovable, black feet.
> 'I will not consider! I have created you and I can create my own heaven.'
> 'You have created it.'
> (p. 196)

God had given Pincher freedom to choose, and all the time his choices had led to the final choice when, in his mad hatred of one of his shipmates, he had ordered the steersman to turn towards the torpedo instead of away from it. But can Pincher be blamed for using the bodies of 'defeated people' as steps by which to climb out of 'the cellar'? Pincher thinks that God is unjust: he is condemned for using the very freedom that God has given him. There is 'no answer' to this contradiction in Pincher's vocabulary, because the terms in which he interprets freedom are those of ruthless self-centredness. He is incapable of understanding the freedom which is a giving of the self to others and to God. His invented self, the self he refuses to surrender, is a creation of misused freedom and a darkening of the image of God in man. It is this invented self that has to be burnt away by the black lightning. God does not leave man in the terrible isolation of his self-delusion. So the lines of divine energy prise open Pincher's predatory claws and penetrate his distorted centre of consciousness 'in a compassion that was timeless and without mercy'.[5]

The isolation of Jesus as he was marched 'outside the gate' on the way to Calvary was not the self-created isolation of a Pincher Martin. In every respect, Jesus was Pincher's opposite. He freely gave himself to others, and his isolation arose from his obedience to the mystery of the Father's will. That obedience meant that Jesus was present for man in his sin as well as in his suffering:

> Christ was innocent of sin, and yet for our sake God made him one with the sinfulness of men, so that in him we might be made one with the goodness of God himself.
> (2 Corinthians 5:21)

Jesus died for the oppressors as well as for their victims; for the exploiters as well as for the exploited; for the prosperous as well as for the wretched of the earth. He absorbed into himself our evil deeds and accepted the judgment of God upon himself as the bearer of them. The measure of human sin is shown to be no less than its power to separate the Son of God from his heavenly Father, to cause a kind of fracture in the Being of

God. The meaning of Calvary cannot be adequately represented as God's punishment of Jesus in order that his suffering and death might satisfy some non-personal moral requirement of the divine will. God did not stand aloof from the cross: he accepted in his Son the dislocation of personal life, the isolating alienation, which is the entail of man's sin and which the cross reveals to us in its undisguised reality. Thus, as Paul puts it, God 'has passed judgment against sin' within our own 'sinful nature' which his Son assumed (Romans 8:3–4): he condemned it and burnt it away, not by an arbitrary external power like Pincher Martin's 'black lightning', but by the fire of his purifying, self-involving love. It is the paradox of God's merciless compassion that T. S. Eliot presents in the well-known lines from *Little Gidding*:

The dove descending breaks the air
With flame of incandescent terror
Of which the tongues declare
The one discharge from sin and error.
The only hope, or else despair
   Lies in the choice of pyre or pyre –
   To be redeemed from fire by fire.

Who then devised the torment? Love.
Love is the unfamiliar Name
Behind the hands that wove
The intolerable shirt of flame
Which human power cannot remove.
   We only live, only suspire
   Consumed by either fire or fire.
   (T. S. Eliot, *Collected Poems 1909–1962*, Faber 1963,
                                      p. 221)

There are, of course, many kinds of 'exile', some of which are more extreme than others. There is the exile of the prisoner; there are the exiles of poverty, discrimination, pain, sickness and old age. There is the exile which can result from the subjection of human life to impersonal economic forces, which have the power, as we say nowadays, to make us 'redundant'. In a poem called 'The Name of the Game', Gavin Ewart derives grim humour from the contrast between the cloudless life of wealthy Mayfair and the insecurity of suburban Bromley:

Today a small agency loses a big account.
It's a fine October day
with a clear sky and sunshine over Mayfair.
The plane trees still have their leaves
still green.

Whisper it gently: Several people
will get the S.A.C.K.
the little death of advertising . . .

What do they tell their wives? There will be
woe in Bromley
As five people fluctuate with the economy.
(In *New Poems 1971–2*, ed. Peter Porter, Hutchinson,
p. 49)

We know a lot about no-man's land in our century, and many of our writers have explored and mapped its various kinds of territory. Exiles, refugees, prisoners of conscience are some of the typical figures of our time. But there are also deeper and more general alienations. No-man's land is not some far-off place: it reaches into our security and into our consciousness — though often we do not fully recognise its presence:

And this Archipelago crisscrossed and patterned that other country within which it was located, like a gigantic patchwork, cutting into its cities, hovering over its streets. Yet there were many who did not even guess at its presence and many, many others who had heard something vague. And only those who had been there knew the whole truth. (*The Gulag Archipelago*, p. x).

Jesus suffered 'outside the gate'. He is one of those who have been there and know the whole truth.

[1] So in the printed text; perhaps a misprint for 'self-censor'?

[2] A. Camus, *The Outsider*, in *The Collected Fiction of Albert Camus*, Hamish Hamilton 1960, pp. 67–68.

[3] Compare the lament over Jerusalem in Luke 19:41–44.

[4] See Reinhold Niebuhr, *Beyond Tragedy* (Nisbet 1938) for an argument in support of this view.

[5] In this section on *Pincher Martin*, I have drawn some material from my essay 'Is Golding's Theology Christian?' published in *William Golding: Some Critical Considerations* by the University of Kentucky Press 1979.

4: Crucifixion

> They brought him to a place called Golgotha, which means 'Place of a skull'. He was offered drugged wine, but he would not take it. Then they fastened him to the cross. They divided his clothes among them, casting lots to decide what each should have.
>
> The hour of the crucifixion was nine in the morning, and the inscription giving the charge against him read, 'The king of the Jews.' Two bandits were crucified with him, one on his right and the other on his left. (Mark 15:22−27)

The gospel record does not dwell on the physical suffering of Jesus. Death by crucifixion was the standard punishment throughout the Roman Empire for rebellion against the State, and it was not in the physical manner of Jesus' death that the gospel writers found the uniqueness of the story they told. Indeed, the torture was the same for the two 'bandits' who were crucified with him. It seems probable that they were members of the band of political rebels (Zealots) mentioned in Mark 15:7 −

> At the festival season the Governor used to release one prisoner at the people's request. As it happened, the man known as Barabbas was then in custody with the rebels who had committed murder in the rising.

These men may have appeared before Pilate's court on the same day as Jesus had done so, since the session would certainly have heard more than one case. So Jesus was 'counted among the outlaws' (Luke 22:37) or 'reckoned among criminals' (Mark 15:27 margin) in the sense that he was crucified in place of one rebel (Barabbas) and in company with two others. Moreover, the inscription 'King of the Jews' signified the political offence of denying the sovereignty of the Emperor (John 19:12). These considerations bring the crucifixion into a political context, even though Pilate had found the political charge against Jesus unsubstantiated and had sought to acquit him.

Crucifixion must have been a hideously painful and humiliating death; but we hardly need to be persuaded in our century that there are circumstances in which human beings will do terrible things to other human beings, and that they do them convinced that their actions are good. It seems that no outrage is so barbarous that it cannot be justified by an appeal to some authority or ideal which is alleged to have an absolute moral claim. The 'final solution' of the Jewish question in Nazi Germany was accommodated with decreasing discomfort by the political myth of the master race, and in the end the willingness to murder Jews could even be regarded as proof of heroism. Nor, on the whole, can it be said that revolutionary and liberation movements are very different: human lives are expendable because all value belongs to the future triumph of the cause; so oppression, betrayal, torture and murder can be justified as the necessary sacrifice of the present reality to the future dream. Solzhenitsyn points out that 'ideology' can justify anything. To do evil, men must somehow persuade themselves that their actions are good. Once they succeed in this, there are no limits to the outrages they will perpetrate against their fellow human beings. Shakespeare's villains, says Solzhenitsyn, never reached this stage of evil-doing. Their imaginations stopped at a dozen corpses — because they had no *ideology*.

Ideology is what gives the evil-doer his justification. That is what enables him to think of his actions as good and to believe that he deserves the praises rather than the reproaches and curses of humanity. Thanks to ideology, the twentieth century has been fated to experience evil-doing 'on a scale calculated in millions':

> That is the precise line the Shakespearean evil-doer could not cross. But the evil-doer with ideology does cross it, and his eyes remain dry and clear.
>
> (*The Gulag Archipelago*, pp. 173–174)

51

The literature of our own time may be said to have made up for Shakespeare's deficiency. We do not have to look far to discover literary examples of ideologically motivated evil-doers who have crossed Solzhenitsyn's line. Here is Rubashov in Koestler's *Darkness at Noon* reflecting on the Communist technique:

> Never in history has so much power over the future of humanity been concentrated in so few hands as in our case. Each wrong idea we follow is a crime committed against future generations. Therefore we have to punish wrong ideas as others punish crimes: with death . . .
>
> We admitted no private sphere, not even inside a man's skull. We lived under the compulsion of working things out to their final conclusions. Our minds were so tensely charged that the slightest collision caused a mortal short-circuit. Thus we were fated to mutual destruction.
>
> (A. Koestler, *Darkness at Noon*, Penguin ed., pp. 100–101)

Another example: Sartre's play *Le Diable et le bon Dieu* has as its central character a land-owning general named Goetz, who acts first on the side of the devil and then on the side of God. Paradoxically, his would-be good actions become the cause of a peasants' revolt and produce far more suffering than his evil actions. Only one possibility remains: to repudiate both God and devil and to take full responsibility for the future pursuit of the war upon himself. The play ends with this resolution:

> I shall fill them with horror since I have no other means of loving them, I shall give them orders since I have no other way of obeying. I shall remain alone with this empty sky above me since I have no other way of being with every-body. There is this war to wage and I shall wage it.

So Goetz takes the fatal step across the line: there is no God, so he will be god. This logic leads inevitably to a political absolut-ism which not merely permits but actually demands a policy of terror.

Once the line has been crossed, the rituals of terror tend to become detached from the ideological myth which justifies them and to be enacted as customs whose origin is only vaguely remembered. Kafka imagines a penal settlement in which torture has become a work of art with no other end than that of a hideous, perverted aestheticism. A machine called The Harrow gradually inscribes more and more deeply into the condemned man's flesh the crime of which he is accused – and which he himself does not know until he reads it in his own wounds:

> The first six hours the condemned man stays alive almost as before, he suffers only pain. After two hours the felt gag is taken away, for he no longer has strength to scream. Here, into this electrically heated basin at the head of the Bed, some warm rice-pap is poured, from which the man, if he feels like it, can take as much as his tongue can lap. Not one of them ever misses the chance. I can remember none, and my experience is extensive. Only about the sixth hour does the man lose all desire to eat . . .
> But how quiet he grows at just about the sixth hour! Enlightenment comes to the most dull-witted. It begins around the eyes. From there it radiates. A moment that might tempt one to get under the Harrow with him. Nothing more happens after that, the man only begins to understand the inscription, purses his mouth as if he were listening. You have seen how difficult it is to decipher the script with one's eyes; but our man deciphers it with his wounds. To be sure that is a hard task; he needs six hours to accomplish it. By that time the Harrow has pierced him quite through and casts him into the grave, where he pitches down upon the blood and water and the cotton-wool. Then the judgment has been fulfilled, and we, the soldier and I, bury him.
> (F. Kafka, 'In the Penal Settlement', in *Metamorphosis and Other Stories*, Penguin Modern Classics, pp.179–180)

The references to the inscription, the sixth hour, and water and blood, suggest that Kafka may have had the crucifixion partly in mind, and that he saw the victim of the Harrow as a twentieth-century example of the same policy of terror as that which nailed Jesus to the cross. And it may be that Jesus, in the six torturing hours of Calvary, like the man under the Harrow, deciphered in *his* wounds the meaning of the inscription – the King of the Jews. Perhaps he deciphered there the mystery of that kingship. He had said to Pilate, 'My kingdom does not belong to this world' (John 18:36) – but the full significance of that conviction could be deciphered only on Calvary. The kingship of Jesus was the kingship of self-giving, the willingness to represent mankind in the passion of man and to plumb that passion to its depths. It had nothing to do with the kingship of political empire or arbitrary power or invulnerable privilege. Jesus had said to his disciples:

'You know that in the world the recognised rulers lord it over their subjects, and their great men make them feel the weight of authority. That is not the way with you; among you, whoever wants to be great must be your servant, and whoever wants to be first must be the willing slave of all. For even the Son of Man did not come to be served but to serve, and to give up his life as a ransom for many.'

(Mark 10:42–45)

The god in whose name political absolutisms claim to govern or to recreate the human race is a mythological god of arbitrary power and unpredictable terror – like Caliban's god 'Setebos' in Browning's poem:

'Thinketh, such shows nor right nor wrong in Him,
Nor kind nor cruel: He is strong and Lord.
'Am strong myself compared to yonder crabs
That march now from the mountain to the sea,
'Let twenty pass, and stone the twenty-first,
Loving not, hating not, just choosing so.
'Say, the first straggler that boasts purple spots
Shall join the file, one pincer twisted off;
'Say, this bruised fellow shall receive a worm,

And two worms he whose nippers end in red;
As it likes me each time, I do: so He.

(R. Browning, Caliban upon Setebos)

But the God to whom Jesus gave his obedience is the diametrical opposite of this mythological god: he is the suffering God, whose kingship is represented by a crown of thorns. The cross therefore brings under condemnation all forms of ideological absolutism, whether established or revolutionary, which justify torture and murder in the name of a divinised human collective, the kingdom of Man:

> 'I leave it to others [says Tarrou in *The Plague*] to make history. I know I'm not qualified to pass judgment on those others . . . All I maintain is that on this earth there are pestilences and there are victims, and it's up to us, so far as possible, not to join forces with the pestilences . . . You see, I'd heard such quantities of arguments, which very nearly turned my head, and turned other people's heads enough to make them approve of murder; and I'd come to realise that all our troubles spring from our failure to use plain, clear-cut language . . . That's why I say there are pestilences and there are victims; no more than that. If, by making that statement, I, too, become a carrier of the plague-germ, at least I don't do it wilfully. I try, in short, to be an innocent murderer. You see, I've no great ambitions.'
>
> (A. Camus, The Plague, Penguin ed., pp. 207–208)

Jesus was not a rebel in the political sense of one who sets himself against the authority of the State; but he *was* a rebel in the sense that his whole life was a fight against the forces which distort the image of God in man. St Luke tells us that he prayed for the soldiers who nailed him to the cross, and that he spoke words of comfort to one of those who were crucified with him (Luke 23:34, 43). In Camus' metaphor, he refused to be 'a carrier of the plague-germ': he accepted the onslaught against himself, but he would not allow it to pass from himself to others. 'He saved others', said some of the bystanders at Calvary, 'but he cannot save himself' (Mark 15:31); but to save others meant a willingness to bear the assault of evil and to be a barrier through which it could not pass. Perhaps there is no other way by which the forces of distortion can be halted.

Writing after the murder of missionaries in Rhodesia in February 1977, a friend of the murdered men showed what resistance to 'the plague-germ' can mean today:

> 'The missionaries are the only whites who do not carry guns' said a newspaper report. That fact contains a multiple significance. Above all, it represents the truth that the human vocation is not the acquisition and exercise of power over others, and that political activity should not be reduced to a decision about who shall kill whom . . . The plain truth is that no political, racial or cultural grouping holds a monopoly of barbarity and violence. The greed for power and the instinct to use cruel means to hang on to it runs across such frontiers . . . The churches' concern is not the maintenance of any political creed, party or system, but the defence of vital human rights and liberties . . . The Church is sorely needed as a resistance movement which defines and bears witness to the true goal of political activity. Its neutrality is active not passive. And the price it pays for the right to sit in judgment is its deliberate abdication of physical power, the willingness of its representatives to meet death without guns in their hands.
>
> (John F. X. Harriott, SJ, *The Times* Feb. 19, 1977)

In this refusal to oppose terror with the weapons of terror, we recognise the spirit of the crucified Jesus. But we may need to be reminded that the Church and its representatives do not always manifest that spirit. Ideological justification of terror is not the monopoly of secular power-structures or revolutionary movements: indeed, modern writers who look for earlier parallels to contemporary policies of terror find a classic example in the work of the Inquisition. The Church can forget that its true identification is with the Christ of Calvary, and can all too readily identify itself with a mythological god of arbitrary power. William Golding has given us a literary example of this in his novel *The Spire*, which, though set in medieval times, provides a parable for our own.

Dean Jocelin has a vision of a great spire added above the crossing of nave and transepts of the cathedral building for which he is responsible. He calls his vision his 'spire of prayer' which pierces every stage of prayer, from the bottom to the top (p. 198). So Jocelin crosses the line: he claims for his vision and for himself as its human agent an absolute authority which justifies ruthless exploitation of the people for whom it is his Christian duty to care. The spire is built, but it rests upon inadequate foundations and is distorted and unsafe. Human lives have been sacrificed to a bogus, perverted ideal: 'I traded a stone hammer for four people', says Jocelin (p. 222) when, on his death-bed, he recognises the destructive folly of his pride. And the heaven for which he now longs is no longer the fulfilment of 'the absolute prayer', but the place of healing and reconciliation which he can enter hand in hand with those he has wronged. In a final vision, the spire of Jocelin's sin is miraculously transformed into the blossoming apple tree of Christ's redemption:

> What is terror and joy, how should they be mixed, why are they the same, the flashing, the flying through panic-shot darkness like a bluebird over water?
> In the tide, flying like a bluebird, struggling, shouting, screaming to leave behind the words of magic and incomprehension −
> *It's like the appletree!*
> (W. Golding, *The Spire*, Faber paperback ed., p. 223)

The distorted spire is a product of the distorted image of God in man. Its twisted shape stands above the earth where all may see its witness to the grotesque mythological god which is man's self-projection upon the universe. So also Jesus on the cross was lifted up from the earth and his tortured figure displayed the power operated by the divinised Roman State. But with this terror there is also a unique, miraculous joy: it is the recognition that the crucified victim of the distorted image of God in man is himself the true image of 'the Love that moves the sun and the other stars':

> The SS hung two Jewish men and a boy before the assembled inhabitants of the camp. The men died quickly but the death struggle of the boy lasted half an hour. 'Where is God? Where is he?' a man behind me asked. As the boy, after a long time, was still in agony on the rope, I heard the man cry again, 'Where is God now?' And I heard a voice within me answer, 'Here he is — he is hanging here on this gallows . . .' (E. Wiesel, *Night*, tr. Stella Rodway, Hill and Wang, New York 1960; quoted by D. Soelle in *Suffering*, DLT 1975, p. 145)

The true witness of the Church is not to a god of arbitrary power but to the God whose image is the suffering figure on Calvary. The rebellion of Jesus against the forces of distortion demanded his presence in the deepest recesses of the human condition, a solidarity with men in their sin and pride and pain without privilege or exemption. And because of Jesus men have sometimes been able to recognise in their own suffering and that of others something of his identification with the universal passion of man. The German Jew, Himmelfarb, in Patrick White's novel *Riders in the Chariot*, seeks by expiating his own guilt to take upon himself the sins of the world and to atone for them. He has betrayed his wife by being away from home when the Gestapo came to arrest her. He never sees her again. He escapes from a death camp and makes his way to Australia, where he lives alone in a cottage and supports himself by a factory job. Although he had been a professor of Mathematics in Germany, he gladly accepts the most humble work he can find. One day, as a joke, some of his workmates 'crucify' him. They lash him to a tree with ropes:

> The Jew had been hoisted as high as he would go on the mutilated tree . . . Hoisted high at the wrists, the weight of the body threatened to cut them through. The arms strained to maintain that uneasy contact between heaven

and earth. Through the torn shirt the skin was stretched transparent on the ribs. The head lolled even more heavily than in life . . . But the eyes were visionary rather than fixed. The contemplative mouth dwelled on some breathless words spoken by the mind.

(P. White, *Riders in the Chariot*, pp. 411–2)

At last the factory manager intervenes and Himmelfarb is brought down from his cross:

Very quietly Himmelfarb left the factory in which it had not been accorded him to expiate the sins of the world.

(p. 418)

No – Himmelfarb had not been able to re-enact the full, unique sacrifice of Christ. But one onlooker had recognised the Christ-figure in the old, crucified Jew. That onlooker was an aborigine – himself, like Himmelfarb, a solitary, an outcast, gifted as a painter but anguished by an inability to understand the meaning of his artistic vision:

Because he was as solitary in the crowd as the man they had crucified, it was again the abo who saw most. All that he had ever suffered, all that he had ever failed to understand, rose to the surface in Dubbo . . . So he understood the concept of blood, which was sometimes the sick, brown stain on his own pillow, sometimes the clear crimson of redemption . . .

(pp. 412–3)

The Christ-figure revealed to Dubbo in the crucified Jew and in his own tormented vision is the Christ who bears the sin of the world, the Christ who carries the burden of man's guilt and pain. It is this recognition that releases the springs of Dubbo's creative genius. He paints two pictures: one is a Deposition from the Cross, which shows Himmelfarb being tended by some women of his acquaintance; the other is a painting of the Chariot of Ezekiel's vision, which, though planned long ago, Dubbo is only now able to finish. The themes of the pictures are death, love, and resurrection − the redemption of the world by Christ, represented through the sacrifice and love of the people Dubbo knows. When the paintings are finished, Dubbo's own sacrifice is completed by death. His paintings are taken to be sold at an auction. People laugh at them and they fetch only a few shillings. Somewhere, perhaps, if they have not been destroyed, they are still waiting to be discovered.

When suffering is appropriated in terms of the sacrifice of Christ, it becomes a representation of the passion of mankind and of the love which bore that passion on Calvary. Like Dubbo's paintings, such love is unrecognised by a world in which power comes from the end of a gun. Through his representatives Christ continues to suffer in that world and to absorb into himself its evil deeds. The Ivory Coast poet Bernhard Dadié thanks God for creating him black and for giving him a body with the shape and strength to carry the world's pain and sorrow:

> I thank you God for creating me black,
> For making of me
> Porter of all sorrows,
> Setting on my head
> The World.
> I wear the Centaur's hide
> And I have carried the World since the first morning.
>
> White is a colour for special occasions
> Black the colour for every day
> And I have carried the World since the first evening.

I am glad
Of the shape of my head
Made to carry the World,
Content
With the shape of my nose
That must snuff the wind of the World
Pleased
With the shape of my legs
Ready to run all the heats of the World.
I thank you God for creating me black
For making of me
Porter of all sorrows.

Thirty-six swords have pierced my heart.
Thirty-six fires have burnt my body.
And my blood on all calvaries has reddened the snow,
And my blood at every dawn has reddened all nature.

Still I am
Glad to carry the World,
Glad of my short arms
   of my long arms
      of the thickness of my lips.
I thank you God for creating me black.
White is a colour for special occasions
Black the colour for every day
And I have carried the World since the dawn of time.
And my laugh over the World, through the night, creates
   the Day.
I thank you God for creating me black.

(*French African Verse*, tr. by John Reed and Clive Wake,
                              Heinemann 1972, pp. 59−60)

5: Darkness and Dereliction

Darkness

> At midday a darkness fell over the whole land, which
> lasted till three in the afternoon . . . (Mark 15:33)

This image of universal darkness is a figuration of the pre-
cosmic darkness in which God's creative word first kindled
the light of life:

> In the beginning of creation, when God made heaven and
> earth, the earth was without form and void, with darkness
> over the face of the abyss, and a mighty wind that swept
> over the surface of the waters. God said, 'Let there be
> light', and there was light; and God saw that the light was
> good, and he separated light from darkness.
>
> (Genesis 1:1–4)

Calvary marks a reversion of creation to the condition of
uncreatedness, a regression from being to non-being, from
cosmos to chaos, from life to death, from light to darkness.
The time-scale of history is pushed back beyond history into
the primordial waste and void out of which God called the
universe into existence. It is as though the long tale of life had
been brought to nothing, as if the toilsome millennia had never
been. The Light of Life is in eclipse, and 'darkling stand(s) the
varying shore o' the world'. And since man is himself a little
world containing as it were in miniature the whole range of its
contraries, he is also represented here. In the crucified Jesus the
Son of Man is present for all mankind at the place of sharpest
negation. The darkness of Calvary is both the pre-cosmic
darkness of the void and the fallen darkness of man's soul.
Jesus, at the centre of that darkness, bears in his own passion
the passion of God and man.

So it must follow that there is no human ordeal of darkness from which Jesus, as Son of Man, is absent. Or, to put it another way, the cross at the centre of the darkened earth is the shape which *our* darkness encloses. To explore that darkness to its heart is to be brought to the foot of the cross, to the heart of God.

'Heart of Darkness' is the title Joseph Conrad gave to a story in which he undertook such exploration. The tale has both a geographical and a spiritual dimension. Geographically, it is a journey from the Thames to the Congo and into the heart of 'the dark continent' — a symbolic exploration back to the primeval, universal darkness which 'civilisation' never dispels:

> The sea-reach of the Thames stretched before us like the beginning of an interminable waterway . . . The air was dark above Gravesend, and farther back still seemed condensed into a mournful gloom, brooding motionless over the biggest, the greatest town on earth.
>
> (J. Conrad, *Heart of Darkness,* Bantam Books, p. 3)

The Thames waterway leads to 'the uttermost ends of the earth', because the waters of the earth all flow into each other and the journey into darkness can start from any point. The Congo is a river through time, 'travelling back to the earliest beginnings of the world', and this figuration of a journey into primeval darkness is fused, in the novel's unitary experience, with the figuration of a spiritual journey into the darkness of the human heart.

The story is told by Marlow, who had been commissioned by a Belgian trading company to replace the captain of a Congo river steamer recently killed by Africans. He finds conditions of mindless colonial brutality and exploitation at their worst. Marlow's loathing of what he sees makes him determined to seek out a company agent named Kurtz, who had come to Africa as an idealist with the aim of 'civilising' the natives. Gradually, the truth about Kurtz is revealed. Under the external 'greatness' of the man — his idealism, his gifts of eloquence and enterprise — there had been something lacking, a hollowness at the centre which the wilderness had penetrated and occupied. From the river steamer Marlow looks through glasses at Kurtz's distant house and sees, with a sudden shock, that what he had taken to be ornamental posts around it are human heads impaled on stakes:

> They [the heads] only showed that Mr Kurtz lacked restraint in the gratification of his various lusts, that there was something wanting in him — some small matter which, when the pressing need arose, could not be found under his magnificent eloquence. Whether he knew of his deficiency himself I can't say. I think the knowledge came to him at last — only at the very last. But the wilderness had found him out early, and had taken on him a terrible vengeance for the fantastic invasion. I think it had whispered to him things about himself which he did not know, things of which he had no conception till he took counsel with this great solitude — and the whisper had proved irresistibly fascinating because he was hollow at the core . . .   (pp. 97–98)

Kurtz had come to conquer the wilderness, but it had conquered him. His idealism had been perverted by power and lust and greed until 'his soul had looked within itself . . . and had gone mad'. Marlow 'tried to break the spell' —

> the heavy, mute spell of the wilderness — that seemed to draw him to its pitiless breast by the awakening of forgotten and brutal instincts, by the memory of gratified and monstrous passions . . . This alone had beguiled his unlawful soul beyond the bounds of permitted aspirations.   (p. 112)

But Marlow could do nothing:

> His was an impenetrable darkness. I looked at him as you peer down at a man who is lying at the bottom of a precipice where the sun never shines.   (p. 117)

The mythological archetype of a darkened earth, of an

encroaching chaos which is pre-rational and anti-human, provides the story of Kurtz with a set of universalising images and
measures its events on a trans-historical scale. Thus the story
becomes a mythology of the Fall of Man. The wilderness
invades the soul: human gifts of intellect and imagination are
perverted to the service of a lawless, self-deifying will, and
naive idealism changes to guilty knowledge. Kurtz recognises
this knowledge just before he dies:

> It was as though a veil had been rent. I saw on that ivory
> face the expression of a sombre pride, of ruthless power,
> of craven terror − of an intense and hopeless despair. Did
> he live his life again in every detail of desire, temptation
> and surrender during that supreme moment of complete
> knowledge? He cried in a whisper at some image, at some
> vision − he cried out twice, a cry that was no more than a
> breath:
> 'The horror! The horror!'   (p. 118)

Kurtz had looked into the heart of his own darkness and had
seen there the darkness of the whole universe:

> . . . I understand better the meaning of his stare, that could
> not see the flame of a candle, but was wide enough to
> embrace the whole universe, piercing enough to penetrate
> all the hearts that beat in darkness. He had summed up −
> he had judged. 'The horror!'   (p. 119)

But perhaps we may say that Kurtz's knowledge was not
after all complete. His stare did not quite penetrate to the very
centre of the darkness. It did not see that the darkness encloses
the shape of a cross on which the horror was once for all
*out*stared. It did not see that no human life and no human heart
can be dark through and through if, at the centre, there is a
light which the darkness cannot overcome. It did not see that
there can be no total eclipse which is without all hope of day if
this is a world which the dayspring from on high has visited.
The Gospel does not minimise the horror of man's perverted
will and evil deeds, and it does not deny the tragic drift of the

world towards darkness and death: rather, it intensifies both to a point at which all evasions and rationalisations are stripped away. Only a tragic reading of life can prepare a great salvation for it, which is why we recognise in tragic art our deepest and most fully encompassing vision. Conrad's novel explores our tragedy, compelling us into the universal darkness which surrounded Calvary. But the Christian reading of life invites us to press more deeply still, until we reach the point beyond tragedy — the point at which we discern in the heart of man's darkness the cross of the Son of God.

Dereliction

> . . . and at three Jesus cried aloud, *'Eli, Eli, lema sabachthani?'*, which means, 'My God, my God, why hast thou forsaken me?' (Mark 15:34)

That was not the voice of quiet acceptance in which there is still some element of consolation. Men and women who have reached the point of conscious extremity in affliction and despair do not speak quietly: they cry out in protest against the intolerable end to which they have come.

> But I will not hold my peace;
> I will speak out in the distress of my mind
> and complain in the bitterness of my soul.
>
> (Job 7:11)

To meditate on the crucifixion is to be drawn into the intolerable reality of the world's pain and despair. The hammer which drove in the nails also shattered the illusory consolations by which we try to distance ourselves from the unbearable fact. Calvary is the place where all human securities fail and all merits are cancelled. To meditate on the crucifixion is to be pressed beyond the limits of what is endurable, to be as one of those to whom 'the sorrows of the world are sorrow, and will not let them rest', to be willing to let the passion of man in Jesus penetrate our evasions.

Look, O Lord, and see
   how cheap I am accounted.
Is it of no concern to you who pass by?
   If only you would look and see:
is there any agony like mine,
   like these my torments
with which the Lord has cruelly punished me
   in the day of his anger?
                              (Lamentations 1:11b−12)

The prophet was expressing the unbearable grief of Jerusalem, shattered by foreign invaders, in a lament which was also Israel's cry of dereliction. Christians have applied that lament to the forsakenness of the crucified Jesus, and it echoes in our minds when we encounter at the cross the tragic extremes of human life:

> We must leave on one side the beliefs which fill up voids and sweeten what is bitter. The belief in immortality. The belief in the utility of sin . . . The belief in the providential ordering of events – in short, the 'consolations' which are ordinarily sought in religion.
>
> Human misery would be intolerable if it were not diluted in time. We have to prevent it from being diluted *in order that it should be* intolerable.
>
> (Simone Weil, *Gravity and Grace*, RKP 1963, pp. 13−14)

The cry of dereliction announces the terminus of the journey into no-man's land. It marks the place at which all human work ceases, the zero-point at which every consolation fails. Jesus did not enjoy some privileged exemption from the full measure of the passion of man: there was no nobility of suffering on Calvary, no reserve of human dignity to moderate the degradation and horror of the scene. The cry of dereliction meant what it said: it was the voice which cries out from the total solitude of physical agony and spiritual despair − the tragic protest which is all that a man is capable of before he is finally reduced to the status of a thing by the loss of all that entitles him to be called human. Jesus bore the sin of the world, and there is nothing noble about sin. It thrust him to the farthest possible distance from God, into the heart of a darkness which, in that moment, eclipsed the light of life. God did not spare his own Son: there were no rescuing angels to intervene. The abyss had to be plumbed to its depths because only so could the full measure of man's need be taken.

It is in its refusal to stand back from the abyss, to distance itself from the intolerable, that tragic art claims its most pressing relevance to the story of the cross. In the last act of *King Lear*, there is a scene in which it seems that the tragedy is to be resolved by an intervention of divine justice. Edmund is unmasked and killed by Edgar; Goneril poisons Regan and then stabs herself. It looks as if the cosmic powers have at last moved into action:

> This judgment of the heavens, that makes us tremble,
> Touches us not with pity,

says Albany. In the end, it seems, the gods call a halt to the progression of madness and outrage. They punish the guilty and vindicate the innocent.

But this consoling cosmology is not the last word of the play. Edmund had ordered the death in prison of Lear and Cordelia. Cordelia was to be hanged and faked as a suicide. Edgar sends in haste to have the murder stopped:

> The gods defend her!

says the pious Albany. But the gods do not defend her. The next line is a stage direction:

> *Enter Lear with Cordelia dead in his arms*[1]

That is the hammer-blow which shatters the comforting cosmology of divine intervention in the human tragedy. Evil has found its victim in the one person whom the cosmic powers, if they existed or if they were just, simply could not have left undefended. But Cordelia is dead because the tragedy cannot

68

be arbitrarily resolved. The tale of woe must be fully told until only the fierce cry of protest is left:

> Howl, howl, howl, howl! O! you are men of stones:
> Had I your tongues and eyes, I'd use them so
> That heaven's vaults should crack. She's gone for ever.
> I know when one is dead, and when one lives;
> She's dead as earth.
>
> (Act V scene 3)

So it was with Jesus. His tale of woe was fully told, and it reached a point at which he cried out to the God who had forsaken him in a voice that would have cracked heaven's vault. The cry of dereliction is the great cry of protest against the annihilating power of alienation and death, a kind of 'rage against the dying of the light', against the irrecoverable waste and loss of human life, which, in our time, has found a notable expression in Dylan Thomas' poem, 'Do not go gentle':

> Do not go gentle into that good night,
> Old age should burn and rage at close of day;
> Rage, rage against the dying of the light . . .
> Good men, the last wave by, crying how bright
> Their frail deeds might have danced in a green bay,
> Rage, rage against the dying of the light . . .
> Do not go gentle into that good night.
> Rage, rage against the dying of the light.
> (Dylan Thomas, *Collected Poems 1934–1952*, J. M. Dent
> 1952)

This tragic protest sounds through the ages, but seldom perhaps more frequently or more intensely than in the literature of our century. Here is George Steiner describing a performance of Brecht's play, *Mother Courage*:

> There comes a moment in *Mutter Courage* where the soldiers carry in the dead body of Schweitzerkas. They suspect he is the son of Courage but are not quite certain. She must be forced to identify him. I saw Helen Weigel act the

scene with the East Berlin Ensemble, though acting is a paltry word for the miracle of her incarnation. As the body of her son was laid before her, she merely shook her head in mute denial . . . As the body was carried off, Weigal looked the other way and tore her mouth wide open. The shape of the gesture was that of the screaming horse in Picasso's Guernica. The sound that came out was raw and terrible beyond any description I could give of it. But, in fact, there was no sound. Nothing. The sound was total silence. It was a silence which screamed and screamed through the whole theatre . . .

(G. Steiner, *The Death of Tragedy*, Faber paperback ed., pp. 353–354).

Mother Courage may remind us that Calvary was also the place of a mother's silent anguish – another aspect of the passion of mankind, which, though undwelt upon by the gospel record, has found its focus here in Christian devotion. In a poem called 'Mary's Song', Sylvia Plath pictures a modern Mary cooking lamb for the Sunday meal. The roasting lamb is transmuted into an image of the Jewish holocaust, of the sorrow and desolation of Mary herself, and of the sacrificial heart of her Son in which all the suffering is contained:

The Sunday lamb cracks in its fat.
The fat
Sacrifices its opacity . . .

A window, holy gold.
The fire makes it precious,
The same fire

Melting the tallow heretics,
Ousting the Jews.
Their thick palls float

Over the cicatrix of Poland, burnt-out
Germany.
They do not die.

Grey birds obsess my heart,
Mouth-ash, ash of eye.
They settle. On the high

Precipice
That emptied one man into space
The ovens glowed like heavens, incandescent.

It is a heart,
This holocaust I walk in,
O golden child the world will kill and eat.
          (Sylvia Plath, *Winter Trees*, Faber 1971, p. 39)

Jesus found words of comfort for his mother, commending her into the keeping of 'the beloved disciple' (John 19:26 – 27). But he found no words of comfort for himself, until, at the very end, he passed through despair and voiced his victory in the cry of death.

---

[1] The word 'dead' does not occur in the stage direction as given in the first folio edition of the play. It was inserted by the 18th-century editor Rowe and seems to have been generally adopted by editors and producers since then. But S. may have intended the actual moment of Cordelia's death to remain uncertain.

6: Death

> Then Jesus gave a loud cry and died. And the curtain of the temple was torn in two from top to bottom. And when the centurion who was standing opposite him saw how he died, he said, 'Truly this man was a son of God.'
>
> (Mark 15:37–39)

Mark does not tell us what words Jesus uttered in his death-cry. Perhaps there were no words, but only an inarticulate shout. The Fourth Gospel has, 'It is accomplished!' (John 19:30), and Luke records 'a loud cry' followed by, or possibly consisting of, the words, 'Father, into thy hands I commit my spirit' (Luke 23:46). There can be no doubt, however, that the gospel-writers intended their readers to understand the death of Jesus as a triumphant one. The cry of death was totally different in quality and meaning from the cry of dereliction. The one was marked by physical anguish and spiritual horror: the other was a shout of completion and victory, and it was followed by signs which confirmed that victory — the rending of the veil of the temple and the witness of the centurion. Matthew's gospel adds further signs of a rather bizarre nature — an earthquake, the opening of tombs and the resurrection of the saints — and makes the centurion's words a response to those signs (Matthew 27:51–54). In Mark, however, the centurion's words are specifically related to the death-cry and death of Jesus, not to the signs that followed. Mark suggests that there was something in the manner of Jesus' death which was of itself sufficient to account for the centurion's witness.

It is, of course, highly unlikely that the centurion recognised Jesus as *the* Son of God in the full sense of the Church's post-resurrection faith; but we may suppose that Jesus died differently from other crucified victims, and that the centurion, to whom no doubt crucifixion was a familiar sight, was sufficiently impressed by that difference to attribute to Jesus an astonishing, God-given power of spirit. The body had been weakened by torture to the point of death, to the point at which the normal victim 'no longer has strength to scream'; but Jesus uttered a loud cry which was like a laugh of joy over the world, a shout which seemed to split the darkened earth with the light of recreated day. And the centurion found the only words which seemed big enough to contain the fullness of the event:

'Truly this man was a son of God.'

Of course, we have no direct knowledge of what happened to Jesus in the short interval between the cry of dereliction and the cry of death. It may have been that in the deepest recess of his being there was an affirming power of life which the horror could not touch, and which, at the moment of physical death, burst into full awareness; or perhaps the Spirit of God pressed into the void of his forsakenness and filled him with the light of new creation, dispelling the horror in an overwhelming consciousness of the Father's love. We cannot know. But what we believe is that Jesus 'tasted death for every man', that 'by his death he destroyed death' and opened for us the way to God 'within the veil'.

We may think that there can be nothing in our own human experience which is comparable with the triumphant death of the Redeemer of the World. Strictly speaking, that must be true. Christian faith perceives here a transcendent fullness of meaning which is unique and unmatchable. Nevertheless, we are not total strangers to the last moments of Calvary. Human beings know that they are mortal and that 'the night's Plutonian shore' marks for them the limits of 'the pendant world'. But they also know that they have 'immortal longings', reaching out in imagination and hope beyond those limits to form a vision of life recreated and eternalised in a deathless realm of spirit. So they have dreamed of a power of life beyond their own powers, able to take up the passion of man into an order of reality in which its worth will be affirmed and its tragedy redeemed.

It is when we turn to the greatest works of art and literature that we discover the most compelling demands of hope. Paradoxically, hope seems to acquire its most compulsive form when the imagination probes man's passion to its deepest recesses. Thus Sophocles probes the tale of Oedipus, from his greatness to his fall and through the weary years of a guilty, curse-ridden life. But the death of Oedipus at the end of his long endurance is not the end of the poet's vision: through and beyond the human passion it reaches out towards a hope, mysterious and awe-inspiring, which invests that death with wonder.

[Oedipus, old and blind, bids farewell to his weeping daughters.]
So they wept, clinging to each other. And when they ended, there was silence; until suddenly a Voice called him, a terrifying voice at which all trembled and hair stood on end. A god was calling to him. 'Oedipus! Oedipus!' it cried, again and again. 'It is time: you stay too long.' He heard the summons, and knew it was from God. [Only Theseus is permitted to witness the death of Oedipus.] When we had gone a little distance, we turned and looked back. Oedipus was nowhere to be seen; but the King [Theseus] was standing alone holding his hand before his eyes as if he had seen some terrible sight that no one could bear to look upon; and soon we saw him salute heaven and earth with one short prayer.

In what manner Oedipus passed from this earth, no one can tell. Only Theseus knows. We know he was not destroyed by a thunderbolt from heaven nor tide-wave rising from the sea, for no such thing occurred. Maybe a guiding spirit from the gods took him, or the earth's foundations gently opened and received him with no pain. Certain it is that he was taken without a pang, without grief or agony − a passing more wonderful than that of any other man.

What I have said will seem, perhaps, like some wild dream of fancy, beyond belief. If so, then you must disbelieve it. I can say no more.
(Sophocles, *The Theban Plays*, tr. E. F. Watling, Penguin Classics, pp. 120–121)

Sophocles, it would seem, does not wish to claim too much for his vision. The sole witness of the death of Oedipus is silent, and the messenger acknowledges that his description may appear as 'some wild dream of fancy, beyond belief'. Yet we do believe. We believe because we have been brought to a point at which the passion of man has become intolerable and because hope arises precisely here, as the irresistible demand of our moral awareness, compelling us to make a venture of faith towards a new beginning, towards a realm of being which is beyond tragedy because it encompasses tragedy within a transfiguring affirmation of love.

But tragic art offers us no easily won consolation for the ordeal of its protagonist. Its vision of hope is tentative and distant compared with the exact immediacy of its knowledge of suffering. The tragic hero enacts the universal passion of man, and each of us discovers himself as a participant in it. The end-term of that passion is death, and it has the power to render our passion 'useless':

> I have wrestled with death [says Marlow in *Heart of Darkness*]. It is the most unexciting contest you can imagine. It takes place in an impalpable greyness, with nothing underfoot, with nothing around, without spectators, without clamour, without glory, without the great desire of victory, without the great fear of defeat, in a sickly atmosphere of tepid scepticism, without much belief in your own right, still less in that of your adversary. If such is the force of ultimate wisdom, then life is a greater riddle than some of us think it to be. I was within a hair's breadth of the last opportunity for pronouncement, and I found with humiliation that probably I would have nothing to say. (p. 119)

But the tragic poet *has* something to say. What he says is that, beyond the limits of human knowledge, there is the possibility of a miracle: his last word is not a verdict of futility on a life of suffering which ends in silence and nothingness, *but* −

Oedipus'

All is well.

And Antigone's

My way is to share my love, not share my hate.

And Lear's

This feather stirs; she lives! if it be so,
It is a chance which does redeem all sorrows
That ever I have felt.

And Kent's

Vex not his ghost: O! let him pass; he hates him
That would upon the rack of this tough world
Stretch him out longer.

And Horatio's

Now cracks a noble heart. Good-night, sweet prince,
And flights of angels sing thee to thy rest!

In these examples of the tragic vision, we feel that, through sacrifice and suffering, our awareness has been enlarged and deepened. There is a sense that evil has been worked through and that new possibilities of reconciliation and fulfilment have been won. A way to transcendence has been opened to us, and the tragic sense of life has become an affirmation of eternal values. Even the darkest tragedy cannot be wholly pessimistic: pessimism does not write tragedies, because it has abandoned belief in man's power to transcend the world of his affliction and to discover the redemption of all sorrows. Tragic art reinforces a capacity we have always possessed – to discern beyond suffering and mortality the miracle of redemption. It is through that capacity that the victory of Christ addresses us and claims our joyful assent. That is why we do not come as strangers to the last moments of Calvary: we already knew that the miracle was possible; now we can believe that it is certain.

There are some who argue that, in the literature of our own time, we do not find the sense of transcendence and redemptive hope which seems to be present in classical tragic drama. Tragedy, it is said, belongs to those ages of faith in which men believed that human life was penetrated and encompassed by supernatural powers which reserved the soul of man for salvation or damnation. But, so the argument goes, our own is a sceptical age: the death of God has been announced, and our art can no longer represent the human condition in the same terms as those assumed by the tragic poets. 'Tragedy', says George Steiner in a well known exposition of this view, 'is that form of art which requires the intolerable burden of God's presence. It is now dead because his shadow no longer falls upon us as it fell upon Agamemnon or Macbeth or Athalie' (*The Death of Tragedy*, p. 353). We may reply, however, that the sense of transcendence which tragedy gives, the sense that reality has a cosmic as well as a historical dimension, is not necessarily the same thing as a religious interpretation of life and does not require specifically religious imagery for its expression. The writers of our century explore the passion of man perhaps with greater intensity and urgency than ever before; and although it may seldom use the religious and mythological framework of classical drama, modern tragedy still has the power to make or imply a statement about life which transcends its tale of woe. Religion and tragic art, however, are alike in this: that each discovers transcendence in a statement of human woe which is without compromise or evasion. The paradox of tragic art is that the very fact of making such a statement can liberate the saving hope. The miracle of redemption is not merely a consoling afterthought added as a postscript to the tale of passion: it arises from the tale itself, from the fact that 'a voice is given the creature for its woe', and it requires no explicit appeal to religious doctrines for its accomplishment. Thomas Mann, however, claims that in this power of tragic art there is a parallel with religion: it is at the point of hope that tragedy begins to pass into religious faith. In his novel *Doctor Faustus*, Mann wrestles with the dilemma of the modern artist — in this case, a musician. How can art, which is essentially concerned with form, the overcoming of chaos, the assertion of an order of meanings and values — how can art be created in an age in which all structures have collapsed under the onslaught of barbarism and war? A composer who still avails himself of such devices as sonata-form and traditional tonality simply fails to measure the scale of modern disintegration, and his music is a banal failure to address the horror of the time. The modern Faust must accept the devil's terms: he must himself plumb the abyss of meaninglessness and despair if his art is to register the deep damnation of the modern condition. The Faustus of Mann's novel is a composer named Adrian Leverkühn,[1] and he writes a Lamentation, an 'Ode to Sorrow' which is like a revocation of the Ode to Joy of Beethoven's Ninth Symphony, sounding the depths of Germany's fall into Nazism, war, and a sense of irredeemable guilt. But, like Sophocles in the tragedy of Oedipus, Mann allows his messenger, at the very end, a tentative, undogmatic voice of hope:

> At the end of this work of endless lamentation, softly, above the reason and with the speaking unspokenness given to music alone, it touches the feelings. I mean the closing movement of the piece, where the choir loses itself and which sounds like the lament of God over the lost state of his world, like the Creator's rueful 'I have not willed it'. Here, towards the end, I find that the uttermost accents of mourning are reached, the final despair achieves a voice, and — I will not say it, it would mean to disparage the uncompromising character of the work, its irremediable anguish to say that it affords, down to its very last note, any other consolation than what lies in voicing it, in simply giving sorrow words; in the fact, that is, that a voice is given the creature for its woe. No, this dark tone-poem permits up to the very end no consolation, appeasement, transfiguration. But take our artist paradox: grant that expressiveness — expression as lament — is the issue of the whole construction: then may we not parallel with it another, a religious one, and say too (though only

in the lowest whisper) that out of the sheerly irremediable hope might germinate? It would be but a hope beyond hopelessness, the transcendence of despair – not betrayal to her, but the miracle that passes belief. For listen to the end, listen with me: one group of instruments after another retires, and what remains, as the work fades on the air, is the high G of a cello, the last word, the last fainting sound, slowly dying in a pianissimo-fermata. Then nothing more: silence, and night. But that note which vibrates in the silence, which is not longer there, to which only the spirit hearkens, and which was the voice of mourning, is so no more. It changes its meaning; it abides as a light in the night.

(Thomas Mann, *Doctor Faustus*, p. 471)

The change of meaning from tragic statement to redemptive hope which Mann expresses through his musician's lament is not itself a shift into a religious dimension of understanding. The lament says as much as tragic art *can* say if it is to be tragic – namely, that human imagination and awareness do not move in only a horizontal dimension, and that tragedy has the power, by its very statement of our passion, to urge us towards transcendence. That is Mann's 'artist paradox', and we may recognise it even in the kind of contemporary literature which portrays the human condition one-dimensionally and explicitly denies transcendence. Sartre's play *Huis Clos* (No Exit) could almost stand as the prototype of this genre. There is no way out of a human condition which is characterised by endless attempts and failures to find a justification of existence. The modern hell of Sartre's play is a world cut off from transcendence in which a man and two women are condemned for ever to seek justification from each other and to experience only a mutual torture. Hell does not need the rack because 'hell is other people'. 'We are together here for ever', says Ines at the end of *Huis Clos*. 'For ever', replies Estelle shouting with laughter, 'my God, that's a good one.' Garcin joins in the laughter, and then there is a long silence. 'All right', says Garcin at last, 'let us continue.' And so the play ends.

There is another well known 'no exit' situation in Beckett's

Waiting for Godot. The two tramps are caught in a deadlock. They wait for the mysterious Godot to come with information and instruction which will give some purpose and meaning to their lives; but Godot never comes and they dare not leave the meeting place lest he arrive during their absence. 'Well', says Vladimir in the last lines of the play, 'shall we go?' 'Yes', replies Estragon, 'let's go'. The play ends with a stage direction: *They do not move.*

The real prototype of this literature of deadlock, however, undoubtedly appears much earlier in our century with the work of Franz Kafka. Sartre, Beckett and their epigones are the heirs of a greater writer whose novels and short stories remain as the classic statement of twentieth-century man's impasse:

> There is a parable which describes this situation very well. The Emperor, so it runs, has sent a message to you, the humble subject, the insignificant shadow cowering in the remotest distance before the imperial sun; the Emperor from his death-bed has sent a message to you alone . . .
>
> The messenger immediately sets out on his journey; a powerful, an indefatigable man; now pushing with his right arm, now with his left, he cleaves a way for himself through the throng . . . But the multitudes are so vast; their numbers have no end. If he could reach the open fields how fast he would fly, and soon doubtless you would hear the welcome hammering of his fists on your door. But instead how vainly does he wear out his strength . . . and if at last he should burst through the outermost gate — but never, never can that happen — the imperial capital would lie before him, the centre of the world, crammed to bursting with its own refuse. Nobody could fight his way through here even with a message from a dead man. — But you sit at your window when evening falls and dream it to yourself.
>
> (F. Kafka, 'The Great Wall of China', in *Metamorphosis and Other Stories*, Penguin Modern Classics, pp. 76–77)

Like Beckett's Godot, Kafka's messenger never comes.

Communication is blocked by the impenetrable mass of twentieth-century man's secular apparatus, which implacably seals off human life from transcendence and entirely fails to redeem the time. Yet even here, in this art of the dead-end, the artist paradox, the voice given the creature for its woe, may imply a meaning which will break the impasse, the existence of a standpoint from which the artist's verdict of deadlock is passed and which is not itself part of that verdict. The tragic statement confesses our inability to advance beyond despair[2] and shows that condition to be intolerable — we know that we cannot live in its terms: the miracle of hope is our necessary exit from the intolerable. So perhaps the dead-end artist has a place among the prophets of redemption for our time: he himself is successful even though his messenger is not. By entering the heart of our darkness and delineating the precise form of our plight, he compels us to dream our dream of hope 'on the other side of despair', where, as Orestes says in Sartre's play *The Flies*, 'human life begins'.

Religious faith, of course, makes stronger assertions than this. It claims that the redemptive hope is more than a doubtful dream. Messengers from eternity *have* got through to the world and have disclosed a reality which affirms our vision. Where religion and the art of deadlock agree is in their recognition of man's own inability to alter the basic conditions of his existence, to lift himself beyond finitude and death. Even his greatest art and his finest civilisations are, in the end, incompleted towers of Babel which can never reach up to heaven.[3] Man may dream his dream of freedom, but his heart knows its bondage to the necessities of time. For his dream to become reality, for his hope to be fulfilled, he requires a message from eternity — a 'point of intersection of the timeless with time', where the deadlock is broken and the tragic time redeemed. Tragic art points beyond its statement of the human passion to a redemptive hope which can find its objective correlate only in the God of religious faith. But tragedy can prepare a way for faith by demolishing the barriers against transcendence, the bogus absolutes which men erect as a 'Great Wall of China' within whose little bounds they can play at being masters of reality. Tragedy can also go further: it can shape its tale of woe within a cosmic framework and extend the range of our awareness into universal magnitudes. Those writers who conclude their work in deadlock and despair, forcing us to open up a kind of do-it-yourself exit into transcendence, are not wholly representative of the artists of our time. There are others who explore the passion of man with an equal realism and intensity, but who also essay the task of symbolising the cosmic dimensions of our awareness. A moving example of this symbolisation occurs in William Golding's description of the carrying out to sea of Simon's murdered body in his novel *Lord of the Flies*:

> Along the shoreward edge of the shallows the advancing clearness was full of strange, moonbeam-bodied creatures with fiery eyes. Here and there a larger pebble clung to its own air and was covered with a coat of pearls. The tide swelled in over the rain-pitted sand and smoothed everything with a layer of silver. Now it touched the first of the stains that seeped from the broken body and the creatures made a moving patch of light as they gathered at the edge. The water rose further and dressed Simon's coarse hair with brightness . . .
>
> Somewhere over the darkened curve of the world the sun and moon were pulling; and the film of water on the earth planet was held, bulging slightly on one side while the solid core turned. The great wave of the tide moved further along the island and the water lifted. Softly, surrounded by a fringe of inquisitive bright creatures, itself a silver shape beneath the steadfast constellations, Simon's dead body moved out towards the open sea.
>
> (W. Golding, *Lord of the Flies*, Faber paperback ed., pp. 169–170)

Golding's use of cosmic imagery in this description − light, sun, moon, world, sea and tide − widens the focus of attention, so that Simon's small, murdered body seems to become part of a vast, numinous penumbra surrounding the finite island on which his life has ended. The effect of this transfiguration is to place Simon's sacrificial death in a context of meaning which transcends the horror of the event. Golding's language is literary, not religious; but we move easily into a religious interpretation of it and feel that Simon's death has opened a way into an order of existence where death changes its meaning and becomes 'a light in the night'.

To widen the focus of attention until tragic experience changed its meaning and became redemptive vision, was a fundamental task of the prophets of Israel. Again and again they locate the nation's history within a cosmic framework of meaning which transcends its tale of woe. The great prophet of the Exile urges his readers to enlarge their awareness to the very boundaries of creation itself. The tragic experience of Israel, condemned to suffer in a strange land, is thus placed in a context which reaches out into the breadth of the earth and the height of the heavens:

> Rain righteousness, you heavens,
> let the skies above pour down;
> let the earth open to receive it,
> that it may bear the fruit of salvation
> with righteousness in blossom at its side.
> All this I, the Lord, have created.

> (Isaiah 45:8)

> Thus says the Lord, the creator of the heavens,
> he who is God,
> who made the earth and fashioned it
> and himself fixed it fast,
> who created it no empty void,
> but made it for a place to dwell in:
> I am the Lord, there is no other.

> (Isaiah 45:18)

Hear me, Jacob,
and Israel whom I called:
I am He; I am the first,
I am the last also.
With my own hands I founded the earth,
with my right hand I formed the expanse of the sky;
when I summoned them,
they sprang at once into being.

(Isaiah 48:12−13)

The prophet's language is more than a literary figuration of transcendence. It is a language of faith in the God who created the infinite spaces, who made the earth and the beings who inhabit it, who controls the whole life of nature, and who alone has power to bring light out of darkness and life out of death. When the events of the Exile are measured on this scale of the universe, their dimensions change: they are seen in terms of Jahweh's creative, redeeming will, reaching back through Israel's history to the points where the timeless intersected time in the mighty acts of the exodus from Egypt, the journey across the desert and the settlement in the Promised Land − back to the very foundation of the world. Thus the prophet revalues the sufferings of the Exile: it becomes possible to see them as part of a dynamic which is not finally under the control of human power or limited to the span of human comprehension. A *new* song can now be sung, in contrast to the old nostalgic songs of loss and regret: it is a song which marks a change of meaning from tragic experience to redemptive hope, a song which celebrates a new understanding of Israel's calling as the servant of the Lord whose destiny is to be a light to the Gentiles and whose privilege is to suffer for the redemption of the world:

> Yet on himself he bore our sufferings,
> our torments he endured,
> while we counted him smitten by God,
> struck down by disease and misery;
> but he was pierced for our transgressions,
> tortured for our iniquities;
> the chastisement he bore is health for us
> and by his scourging we are healed.
>
> (Isaiah 53:4−5)

In the New Testament, the redemptive calling of Israel has been fulfilled by one person − Jesus Christ. But he is more than a messenger or agent of eternity: he is the eternal Love itself, who carried love into the deepest recesses of man's sin and despair and whose death opened the way into newness of life in the being of God. It is the cosmic dimensions of the love of Christ that dominate St Paul's prayer for the Christians at Ephesus:

> With deep roots and firm foundations, may you be strong to grasp, with all God's people, what is the breadth and length and height and depth of the love of Christ, and to know it, though it is beyond knowledge. So may you attain to fullness of being, the fullness of God himself.
>
> (Ephesians 3:18–19)

The hopes and dreams which man projects beyond the tragic entail of time are not fated to die in a meaningless universe. They are taken up into a mystery which affirms and yet always transcends them − the mystery of the multidimensional love of God in Jesus Christ.

Tragic art has the power to extend our vision into the breadth and length and height and depth of the cosmos, which, in Christian faith, is filled with the redeeming love of God in Jesus Christ. One of the most unbearable effects of suffering is the isolation of the sufferer within the blank, opaque walls of an imprisoned and fragmented self-hood. The solitude of sickness, bereavement, old age; the loneliness of rejection and disappointed hope; the approach of the final isolation of death

– these are things that drain away 'the courage to be' and reduce human beings to despair. But tragic art is a work of love which removes the isolating walls: it opens up our vision in the horizontal as well as the vertical dimension; it invites us to consider the universal passion of man. It is as though the writer were saying to us, 'Here is suffering; here is evil, conflict, horror and death: come – share it as a sacrifice with me, and together we may find a fellowship which frees us from our prison and turns our faces towards a wider world':

> What do you think refugees do from morning to night? [asks the Italian poet and novelist Ignazio Silone]. They spend most of their time telling one another the story of their lives. The stories are anything but amusing, but they tell them to one another, really, in an effort to make themselves understood. As long as there remains a determination to understand and to share one's understanding with others, perhaps we need not altogether despair.
>
> (I. Silone, 'The Choice of Comrades', in *Encounter*, December 1954).

So also tragedy tells its tale of woe to make us understand that without love there is no cosmos, but only a no-man's land of isolated, fragmentary selves.

In Pasternak's novel about the Russian revolution and its aftermath, Yury Zhivago tells his story of the time in notes and poems. A work of art, he writes, can appeal to us in all sorts of ways – by its theme, subject, situations, characters. But the essence of art is to be found in none of these. What matters is the universalism of art, its power to make 'a statement about life' which draws the multitude of life's contradictions into a unified whole – in a word, its power to create a cosmos. Pasternak's own novel is such a work of art. Its 'statement about life' is of a universe which wills its own harmony in Yury's and Lara's love. Long after they have parted, Lara learns of Yury's death and keeps vigil by his coffin. She thinks back to the happy time of their life together. It seemed as though their love had been created in them by the universe itself, that it was a response to the trees and clouds and sky and earth around them. Even the strangers they passed in the street, the landscapes of their walks together, the very rooms in which they lived, seemed to have taken a delight in their love even greater than their own. Never had they lost this sense of joy in the whole universe, of being part of it and sharing in its form and beauty. That was why, Lara remembers, they had never been attracted by an ideology which exalts man above the rest of nature and sets him up as an object for worship.

But the lesson of Lara's and Yury's love had been that their joy in the whole universe was inescapably tragic. It was the discovery that the highest form of love is the willingness to sacrifice life in order that new live may be born, and that to be part of the love of the universe is to participate in the suffering which all men share. Yury himself expressed this awareness in one of his poems:

> I feel for each of them
> As if I were in their skin,
> I melt with the melting snow,
> I frown with the morning.
> In me are people without names,
> Children, stay-at-homes, trees.
> I am conquered by them all
> And this is my only victory.
> (B. Pasternak, *Dr Zhivago*, Fontana edition, pp. 531–532)

The love of one's neighbour, as Nikolai says early in the novel, is 'the supreme form of living energy': it represents man's greatest attempt to solve the enigma of death. It is linked with 'the ideas of free personality and of life regarded as sacrifice'. These ideas, which, says Nikolai, were bequeathed to the world by Christ, control the pattern of Pasternak's whole novel. Precisely because Yury's and Lara's love opens up to them the cosmic love by which the universe is given form and order, so their personal love must be sacrificed in order that 'the secret stream of suffering may warm the cold of life', in order that the post-revolutionary life of the Russian people may be nourished by the living energy of love of neighbour.

Pasternak explores the inhumanity, the disruption and devaluation of personal life brought about by the revolution, and the disappointed hopes of its aftermath. But the deepest hope does not fail: it is the hope that the suffering will be part of the sacrifice by which love brings renewal and joy to the life of the world.

The New Testament teaches that Christ did more than bequeath ideas to the world. His death was the culmination of a life which had been marked throughout by love of neighbour, and which had brought him, in the end, to the point beyond which no further sacrifice is possible:

> 'There is no greater love than this, that a man should lay down his life for his friends.' (John 15:13)

But that sacrifice could be appropriated by men as a power which would transform their lives. It enabled them to share with Jesus in the passion of mankind, to discover, in the fellowship of Christ's sufferings, something of his freedom from the self-concerned life which imprisons men in anxiety and despair. St Paul could even claim that his own sufferings helped to complete

> the full tale of Christ's afflictions still to be endured, for the sake of his body which is the church.
> (Colossians 1:24)

But there is in the Gospel an opening into a still wider liberty, an enlargement of awareness beyond the passion of man into a reality which redeems our tragedy and affirms an eternal worth in all our finite striving. The Christian way of experiencing this transcendence is through the triumphant death and resurrection of Jesus as Son of God, when fellowship in the suffering of the Son of Man becomes fellowship in the Father's love, filling the void of our forsakenness with the light and life of new creation.

For I am convinced [writes St Paul] that there is nothing in death or life, in the realm of spirits or superhuman powers, in the world as it is or the world as it shall be, in the forces of the universe, in heights or depths — nothing in all creation that can separate us from the love of God in Christ Jesus our Lord.

(Romans 8:38–39)

---

[1] The composer in Mann's novel is modelled on Arnold Schoenberg, who wrote twelve-tone music as Leverkühn does in the novel. Schoenberg did not think that Mann understood this method of composing — which is not, perhaps, surprising. But Schoenberg's rather caustic criticism of Mann's musical understanding does not invalidate the novelist's exploration of the dilemma faced by the 20th century artist.

[2] It was remarkable how a performance of *Waiting for Godot* some years ago in the rather unusual setting of a theological college chapel seemed to emphasise this 'confessional' aspect of the play.

[3] For a classic statement of this view, see Reinhold Niebuhr's essay, 'The Tower of Babel', in *Beyond Tragedy*.

7: Resurrection

On the third day, Jesus rose from the dead. The gospels vary in their accounts of the resurrection. Matthew has a characteristic earthquake and a descent of an angel from heaven. Luke mentions the presence of two men in dazzling garments, and John records two angels in white sitting in the empty tomb. Mark has 'a youth sitting on the right-hand side, wearing a white robe'. But not even Matthew's account, which is the most dramatic of the four, can be said to add up to an overwhelming theophany on the world's stage. In the Fourth Gospel, the description seems to be deliberately *un*dramatic: it is as if the writer were playing down the sheer wonder of the event, as if he were saying that the humility which had marked the earthly life of the Son of Man also marked the resurrection of the Son of God. Mary of Magdala, he tells us, thought at first that Jesus was the gardener.

There is a striking absence of dramatic extravagance in all the accounts of the resurrection appearances of Jesus. Again, the gospels vary in the incidents they report. Jesus appears quite casually in the settings of ordinary life − in the garden, by the lakeside, on the road to Emmaus, in the upper room in Jerusalem. On three occasions we are told that he was at first unrecognised. There is an emphasis on the disciples' slowness to believe, and mention is made of their joy when they saw the Lord.

This restraint in the accounts of the resurrection appearances maintains a characteristic of the whole of the gospel story. Throughout his public ministry, Jesus had consistently refused to present people with compelling displays of divine power: he rejected the temptation to throw himself from the pinnacle of the temple, and his works of healing were acts of compassion rather than deeds of wonder. Men were not to be won for God's kingdom by abrupt and abnormal interventions in the routines of life. The signs of the kingdom were present, for those with eyes to see, in quite ordinary events: in the growth of seed, in the leavening of dough, in the love of a father for his returning son, in the concern of a shepherd for a lost sheep and of a woman for a lost coin. It would be surprising if this characteristic restraint of Jesus' teaching and ministry had been as it were abandoned in the case of the resurrection. Of course, the resurrection *was* an astonishing, a unique event, and the New Testament blazes with the conviction that it has happened; but as Paul discovered when he spoke to the Athenians, the telling of the event was not of itself enough to elicit the response of faith. The deep recesses of a man's being, the world of his experience and relationships, the tensions, conflicts and aspirations of his day-to-day existence — none of these levels of human reality can be reached by an event which is, by definition, wholly outside the normalities of life. It is out of keeping with the entire emphasis of the gospel story to suppose that the resurrection was a kind of one-off, knock-down demonstration of divine power, which, by its very abnormality, would bring the world to the feet of Christ. That was not Jesus' way of winning the world for God. Men quickly forget a nine-days-wonder which has no connection with the persisting conditions of their existence. 'If they do not listen to Moses and the prophets they will pay no heed even if someone should rise from the dead' (Luke 16:31).

The central importance of the resurrection does not derive from the sheer wonder of the event, but from the light which it throws on the whole story of Jesus, and, in consequence, on the life of man in the world. Stated briefly, it meant that what had happened to Jesus on Calvary had also happened in the being of God, that the passion of the Son of Man in the finite world of space and time had also been the passion of the Son of God in the eternal reality of the divine life. The resurrection reshaped a story of human tragedy into the story of God's supreme work of salvation. God had raised Jesus from the dead, and this unique event implied that Jesus possessed a unique relationship with the Father in heaven. As Son of Man, Jesus had identified himself with the passion of mankind to the point of crucifixion and death; but as Son of God, he had taken our alienated humanity into the eternal life of God, into the loving relationship between God the Father and God the Son, in which human sin was absorbed and overcome by the transfiguring energy of the divine love. The writer to the Hebrews expresses this in terms of the Jewish model of sacrifice: Jesus offered himself in sacrifice to God, but his offering was not presented in the earthly sanctuary 'made by men's hands which is only a symbol of the reality'; Christ has entered 'heaven itself, to appear now before God on our behalf' (Hebrews 9:24). The 'real' sanctuary, the true 'holy of holies', is nothing other than the being of God himself, and it was there, within the mystery of the divine reality, that Christ on our behalf offered the sacrifice of his life. The risen body still bore the marks of the nails and spear: the wounds caused by sin had healed, but the scars remained engraved upon the hands and feet and side as a figuration in history of God's eternal appropriation of the passion of man in his Son. 'Behold, I have graven you on the palms of my hands', said Jahweh to Zion in Second Isaiah's great prophecy (Isaiah 49:16 RSV): in the risen body of Christ, that prophecy was seen to be true; but the engraving had been done by men, and God in Christ had accepted the wounds in order to heal them and to make that healing manifest in the world.

The resurrection connects with human life through the story of the Son of Man, who was present for man at every point of his tragedy and hope. It tells us that tragedy is not the last word of life, that sin and evil are not part of the final truth of the universe, but that the creative Power which brought the world into being is able to absorb and overcome the evil which that world has produced. So man is led towards a hope which is at the same time a disclosure of responsibility: the fault is not in his stars, but in himself; he cannot blame life or God for the tragedy which is of his own making, contingent upon the sin which he commits in his misused freedom; what he sees as the inevitable drift of the world towards darkness and death is a projection on to the world of the darkness and death in his own soul. But to see the world under the aspect of resurrection is to see it transfigured by the light and life of the Son of God, who, as the man on the cross, witnessed to the possibility that love can be present even in circumstances which seem to cry aloud its impotence and defeat. The resurrection takes that possibility and makes of it the master-light of all our seeing, revealing the essential reality of life in and beyond the tragic history of man in the world. So man cannot now curse God and die: he must accuse himself and be led to repentance and faith. Life is not meaningless and its defeats are not final if the tragic defect is in man himself. 'If we can only weep for ourselves as men', says Reinhold Niebuhr, 'we need not weep for ourselves as man.'

So perhaps we may use a literary analogy, and say that Easter transformed the human tragedy into the *divine comedy*: not, of course, as something for shallow amusement, but in the sense of the title of Dante's great poem as the joyful recognition of the fact that tragedy has been transcended by 'the Love that moves the sun and the other stars'. Man's age-old lament over the stigma of his mortality has become the Lord's song of triumph over the new birth of his creation. We learn here that life is stronger than death and love is stronger than hate and hope is stronger than despair. The miracle beyond tragedy has happened, and no part of the passion of man lies outside the redeeming, eternalising power of resurrection. The Easter faith is the faith that the cross at the centre of the darkened earth is the cross not only of the Son of Man but also of the Son of God. Wherever on this earth there is sin and suffering and despair and death, there is the cross of the Son of Man; and wherever the cross is, there also is the power of the resurrection of the Son of God. Whenever man utters his age-old lament over the stigma of his mortality, then also the risen Christ gives the word of healing and eternal life. The statement of the human tragedy is answered by the counter-statement of the divine comedy: 'In the world you have tribulation; but be of good cheer, I have overcome the world' (John 16:33 RSV).

It does not seem to be possible to understand the meaning of the resurrection if we think of the event as an arbitrary intervention in human history comparable to that of the god from the machine who appeared at the end of some of the old Greek dramas in order to extricate the characters from the otherwise insoluble dilemmas of the plot. The Easter faith does not trivialise life by removing from it the tragic entail of man's striving; rather, it identifies for us the life-affirming presence of God in the persisting realities of existence — the love which constantly seeks to draw evil into itself and to elicit even from extremes of suffering and loss the values which enable men to live in hope. The resurrection sensitises us to those elusive signals of transcendence which come through the ongoing, day-to-day circumstances of our life, and we know that they are not merely self-deceiving attempts to conceal from ourselves the baleful truth that our existence is unjustified and our passion useless. We know them now as signals of resurrection, as manifestations in time of the eternal redemption wrought in the being of God. The risen Christ appears to us as he appeared to the disciples, in humility, in quietness, bearing the marks of his self-involvement in the abrasive reality of human life and revealing to us the healing power of divine salvation. He appears at those points where we see love answering hate, compassion answering suffering, forgiveness answering outrage, affirmation of life answering its denial; he appears both as the victim of the human passion and as its redeemer, calling us to count ourselves on his side in our own commitment and witness to the world.

Like the disciples, however, we often do not recognise the presence of the risen Christ in these familiar patterns of life. Signals of death seem to dominate the world: they come over loud and clear, so that signals of resurrection are drowned. We hear the statement of the human tragedy, but the counter-statement of the divine comedy is faint and distant and easy to miss. The word of life becomes inaudible amid the unabating clamour of the words of death. We have tried in this book to listen to those words of death through some of the literature of our time and to hear in them the passion of the Son of Man who suffered and died on Calvary. We have followed the tragic journey of Jesus through his agony, his arrest and trial, his condemnation, rejection, forsakenness and death, and we have seen how that journey is re-enacted in the experience and the consciousness of man in our own century. We have noticed the tragic irony of the cheering and rejoicing which marked the entry of Jesus into Jerusalem on the first Palm Sunday, when the crowds hailed him as the triumphant Son of David, and we have been put in mind of many hopeful journeys by which man in our time has unwittingly entered into his passion. Yet the Church today still keeps Palm Sunday, as it has always done, as a day of celebration and triumph. We have not changed it into a day of mourning for one whose crown turned out to be a crown of thorns, though we do mourn over the sin which made that crown. For we know that the journey did not end on Calvary: we know that on the third day Jesus rose again, that the wounds of his passion were healed, and that through him God spoke the word of life which gives to the world the message of eternal redemption.

Is that word of life also present in the experience and consciousness of man in our time? We have heard many words of death, and often it seems that the message of redemption no longer reaches us. Yet we have found that tragic literature is itself a work of love, which, by entering and defining our plight, conveys to us 'the sharp compassion of the healer's art', and we have recognised there the presence of the crucified Son of Man. But does our art also help us to recognise the risen Son of God? Does it reveal to us the healing of the wounds of passion? Does it enable us to hear the word of life which transforms the human tragedy into the divine comedy?

In William Golding's novel *Free Fall*, the hero, Sammy Mountjoy, is taken prisoner by the Germans and shut up in a cupboard normally used to store cleaning materials. Sammy does not know what kind of 'cell' he is in, and his imagination fills it with the horrors of a nightmare. He cries out for help like a rat shaken by a terrier: 'I cried out not with the hope of an ear but as accepting a shut door, darkness and a shut sky' (p. 184). But 'the thing that cried out came up against an absolute helplessness'. Physical escape was impossible, but what Sammy was fighting for was his soul: the real struggle was inside himself, in the destructive darkness which throughout his life had gradually invaded the centre of his being. 'The thing that screamed left all living behind and came to the entry where death is close as darkness against eyeballs.' (p. 185). And at that moment of supreme horror Sammy 'burst that door': his being broke through the darkness of death and emerged into the light of life.

When Sammy is at last released from his cell, he walks through the prison camp like 'a man resurrected'. All around him, in the huts and the wire and in the mountains beyond, he sees affirmation of life, reaching out beyond his physical surroundings to 'the movement of the earth and sun and unseen stars . . . the business of the universe proceeding there in its own mode, different, indescribable . . . like a burst casket of jewels':

> Standing between the understood huts, among jewels and music, I was visited by a flake of fire, miraculous and pentecostal; and fire transmuted me, once and for ever.
> (W. Golding, *Free Fall*, Faber paperback ed., p. 188)

But Sammy's vision of the glory of the world is in terrible contrast with his awareness of himself: his interior identity seems to produce loathsome shapes which fly outwards along 'the radii of the globe'. 'The light that showed up this point and these creatures came from the newly perceived world in all its glory' (p. 190). So Sammy is no longer content to live with his own nature, and his experience of a world reborn leads him to search his life to find the moment when he fell from the freedom of his boyhood acceptance of all existence into the condition of alienation and destruction which had brought him finally to the darkness and horror of the cell. Sammy is an artist, and he tries to paint the transfigured prison camp, the 'new world' of his changed vision. But he is not successful. One or two of his paintings 'see the dust and the wood and the concrete and the wire as though they had just been created. But the world of miracle I could not paint then or now' (p. 189). What he must do is to become part of the new world, to adapt the nature of 'the dead thing' which is himself so that it will conform to the reality which can raise it into life.

Sammy could not paint the miracle of resurrection. He was also aware of the fact that words cannot tell the whole truth – 'language is clumsier in my hands than paint'. No doubt Golding himself is speaking here, telling the reader how hard it is to express in words the experience of a world transfigured and a soul reborn. Perhaps that is why some writers appeal to *music* when they seek an image of conflict resolved and life affirmed. Music can resolve all its dissonances into what Robert Browning calls 'the C Major of this life', and we have the feeling that we have journeyed through the travails of existence and have finally arrived at a place where the soul is truly at home. One of the most famous examples of this is the finale of Beethoven's fifth symphony, of which E. M. Forster has a celebrated description in his novel *Howards End*. Helen Schlegel, a central character in the novel, is listening to a performance of the work in Queen's Hall. The opening of the scherzo makes her think of

> a goblin walking quietly over the universe from end to end. Others followed him. They were not aggressive creatures; it was that that made them so terrible to Helen. They merely observed in passing that there was no such thing as splendour or heroism in the world.

But the 'goblins' are scattered by the triumphant C Major of the finale. Beethoven

> gave them a little push, and they began to walk in a major key instead of in a minor, and then − he blew with his mouth and they were scattered.

And although the goblins return in the finale when the theme of the scherzo suddenly reappears,

> Beethoven chose to make all right in the end. He blew with his mouth for the second time, and again the goblins were scattered. He brought back the gusts of splendour, the heroism, the youth, the magnificence of life and death, and, amid vast roarings of a superhuman joy, he led his Fifth Symphony to its conclusion.

Helen leaves the building after the performance of the symphony:

> The music had summed up to her all that had happened or

could happen in her career. She read it as a tangible statement, which could never be superseded.

(E. M. Forster, *Howards End*, Penguin ed., pp. 46–47)

Her sister Margaret is critical of Helen's penchant for labelling music with meanings and turning it into literature (p. 52); Margaret herself prefers music to be treated as music, as a language in its own right which does not require translation into words. But Helen's interpretation of Beethoven serves Forster well both as an indicator of Helen's optimistic cast of mind and as a kind of preview of the events which are to follow. The 'goblins' do indeed walk across Helen's world; and although the conclusion of the novel hardly matches the triumphant ending of the symphony, nevertheless it suggests that the goblins have been dispelled, if only temporarily, and that Howards End and the people who now live in it have arrived at their own 'C Major' of affirmation and hope.

Browning's phrase, 'the C Major of this life', comes from his poem *Abt Vogler*, in which a musician soliloquises as he plays an improvisation on the organ. Abt Vogler claims that musicians can go directly to the source of values:

Sorrow is hard to bear, and doubt is slow to clear,
Each sufferer says his say, his scheme of the weal and woe:
But God has a few of us whom he whispers in the ear;
The rest may reason and welcome: 't is we musicians
  know.

But Browning's musician still requires words to explain the meaning of the sounds he creates — words which identify the music as a signal of resurrection, as an assurance that the power which expands the musician's heart is the power of God, and that the music rises beyond its extinction in time to a reality which appropriates and eternalises it. So in Browning's poem music becomes the bearer of a faith which exists independently of it and which leads the poet into a general statement of the eternity of all values:

There shall never be one lost good! What was, shall live as
    before;
The evil is null, is nought, is silence implying sound;
What was good shall be good, with, for evil, so much
    good more;
On the earth the broken arcs; in the heaven, a perfect
    round.

All we have willed or hoped or dreamed of good shall
    exist;
Not its semblance, but itself; no beauty, nor good, nor
    power
Whose voice has gone forth, but each survives for the
    melodist
When eternity affirms the conception of an hour.
                 (R. Browning, *Abt Vogler* ix and x)

In a rather similar way, T. S. Eliot finds in music a figuration
of ultimate harmony, identifying one of those moments 'in
and out of time' when we apprehend eternity:

        . . . music heard so deeply
That it is not heard at all, but you are the music
While the music lasts.
      ('The Dry Salvages', *Collected Poems 1909 – 1962*)

Such moments are, however, only 'hints and guesses': it is in
the light of the Gospel that we understand their meaning. The
poet goes on to say that Christ united in himself the two
'spheres of existence', the great opposites of past and future,
which include time and eternity, death and resurrection. What
we hear in the music is a hint of the harmonisation of life
accomplished in the being of God by him who, for our sake,
died and rose again. 'We had the experience', as Eliot says
earlier in the poem, 'but missed the meaning'. When we
approach the meaning, the experience is restored 'in a different
form, beyond any meaning we can assign to happiness'. It is no
longer merely a fugitive sense of well-being, but a lasting
awareness of the victory of Christ, which, though always

transcending our life on earth, nevertheless nourishes through us 'the life of significant soil'.

Another writer who hears in music the language of eternity is the contemporary dramatist Peter Shaffer. The music in this case is that of Mozart, and the thesis of Shaffer's recent play is derived from Mozart's middle name, *Amadeus*, which means 'loved by God'. The composer Salieri, who, according to legend, is supposed to have poisoned Mozart, recognises in the supreme genius of his rival's compositions the transmission of a supernatural power of which, in Salieri's view, the human Mozart is quite unworthy to be the channel. We know from his letters that Mozart was fond of billiards and dancing, and that he sometimes indulged in scatalogical humour. Salieri, in Shaffer's play, finds it intolerable that such a trifler should have been chosen by God to be the instrument of the music of eternity, beside which Salieri's own music is that of a merely human talent. The rivalry between the two men is based, not upon their relative success in the musical life of Vienna (historically, Salieri seems to have been the more popular of the two), but upon the difference between an inspired genius and a worthy plodder; and it is his appreciation of this difference which, in Shaffer's play, motivates the jealousy and hatred of Salieri.

The psychology of the play depends upon the acceptability of the premise that the name 'Amadeus' represents literal truth: namely, that Mozart was a composer whom God whispered in the ear, that he was a channel by which Eternity conveyed eternity to the world. 'God *needed* Mozart, do you see, to let himself into the world', says Salieri in the play. Of course, we do not have to accept Salieri's excessive idea that Mozart was merely a human pipe-line through which the music came from God ready-made. Artistic inspiration does not work like that. But at its greatest Mozart's music does seem to express an affirmation and a transfiguration of life which some of us feel comes closer than any other art to the 'divine comedy' which the New Testament calls 'resurrection' – closer, for example, than the loud drama of Mahler's 'Resurrection' symphony or Messiaen's 'Et Exspecto'. 'Whatever else shall pass away', says Salieri after hearing a performance of

The Marriage of Figaro, 'this must remain.' And Peter Shaffer, writing his play for a sceptical age dominated by words of death, *knows that we will agree.*

Perhaps the insight of Shaffer's play is that the resurrection vision is always a miracle: we cannot command its presence or prescribe the circumstances in which it will occur. It comes to us as an unexpected grace in conditions which often seem to be 'unpropitious'. Our best and only hope is that when we hear the word of life we shall recognise it for what it is.

On one of the black days of our century in September 1968, the Warsaw Pact countries sent troops into Czechoslovakia and Russian tanks rolled into Wenceslas Square to bring Dubcek's 'Prague Spring', his 'Socialism with a human face', to an end. On the following evening, by one of those ironies which sometimes occur in history, the Russian cellist Rostropovich was playing the Dvořák cello concerto with the Soviet State Orchestra at a promenade concert in the Albert Hall in London. There was some heckling from the audience as the players entered, but it died away when the music began. It was immediately apparent that the real protest against the events in Prague was coming from the concert platform, not from the audience. Soloist and orchestra played like men possessed. And as they recreated the music of the greatest Czech composer, the feeling of irony and bitterness faded: it was replaced by a sense of resurrection. A counter-statement was being made to the statement of death, and it spoke of a life that is stronger than death and of a freedom that is stronger than oppression.

No doubt it was easy for us, who were listening to the music in London, to feel in this way. But a concert in London, it may be said, made no difference to the tragic events in Prague. Of course, that is true. Resurrection promises no immediate victories and the wounds of our calvaries do not heal in three days. But what we heard in the music was the word of life, and it did not seem impossible to believe that, in some way, the Czechs might hear it too.

It remains to add that the New Testament does not understand resurrection only as a new way of seeing the world. What man needs is not only a transformed vision but also a transformation of himself and his actions. He is meant to be more than a spectator of the divine comedy: he is invited to take part in it as a *performer*, to act out the drama of redemption in his own life and in the circumstances of his time. The resurrection gave the disciples of Jesus a new vision and a new hope; but it was not until the pentecostal fire came upon them that they received the power to live out that vision and that hope in the world. The Spirit of God, through whom Christ offered his eternal sacrifice to the Father, imparted to the disciples 'the spiritual energies of the age to come' (Hebrews 6:5) by which they were enabled to live and speak and act as witnesses to the redemptive victory of the risen Lord. Those who were later called 'Christians', who had accepted Christ as Lord and were conscious of having received the Spirit in baptism, spoke of their new life as 'resurrection'. It was as if they had died with Christ and risen again with him into a new age marked by forgiveness of sins, fellowship in the community of the Church, and a recreating energy of life which made them 'more than conquerors' in a world of tribulation.

Writing in a CMS News-Letter, Simon Barrington-Ward takes us back to the beginning of the Gospel story – as the Church has done year by year down the centuries:

> Advent and Christmas draw us onward through the shortened days and the closing in of the dark, towards a border country, a country where opposites may mingle, a no-man's land that belongs to every man. In our search for a fundamental purpose and meaning in the world, a true shape to society, and adequate forms of thought and feeling and personal life, we can I believe be grasped, if we would go willingly to the place where creations are humbled to receive a power which meets their need. The power meets the need of/disintegrated societies, changing religions, fragmentary and seemingly inconsequential lives, because they are essentially the needs of persons. And it is a personal love which can heal and recreate, and carry us through and beyond the contradictions of finitude and death into a boundless future, as together in the mysterious phrase of the Gospel we 'become the Son

of Man'. (S. Barrington-Ward, *CMS News-Letter*, December 1975)

When we follow through the Gospel story to its end, we learn that to 'become the Son of Man' is to share in the passion of mankind through the passion of the man on the cross. What we experience in that identification is a liberation from the self-concerned life which locks us inside our fragmented self-hood — a strange and terrible liberation into the whole universe of human woe, into 'a no-man's land that belongs to every man'. Man's tragic art is the form in which the creative imagination expresses and enacts the universal woe which the Son of Man appropriated in its full actuality: it helps us to enter as participants into the tragic drama of Calvary. But Calvary is also the way to the resurrection beyond tragedy, to the divine comedy which opens to us a power of love which bears our guilt and pain and loss into the being of God, a power of goodness which burns away sin and blots out evil, a power of life which transforms the passion of man into the redeeming victory of the Son of God. That is the Gospel — the word of life that declares to us 'the life which we share with the Father and his Son Jesus Christ':

It was there from the beginning; we have heard it; we have seen it with our own eyes; we have looked upon it, and felt it with our own hands; and it is of this we tell. Our theme is the word of life. This life was made visible; we have seen it and bear our testimony; we here declare to you the eternal life which dwelt with the Father and was made visible to us. What we have seen and heard we declare to you, so that you and we together may share in a common life, that life which we share with the Father and his Son Jesus Christ. And we write this in order that the joy of us all may be complete. (1 John 1:1–4)

Index of Authors/Composers